Java™ Essentials for C and C++ Programmers

Java™ Essentials for C and C++ Programmers

Barry Boone

Addison-Wesley Developers Press
Reading, Massachusetts • Menlo Park, California • New York
Don Mills, Ontario • Harlow, England • Amsterdam
Bonn • Sydney • Singapore • Tokyo • Madrid • San Juan
Paris • Seoul • Milan • Mexico City • Taipei

Many of the designations used by manufacturers and sellers to distinguish their products are claimed as trademarks. Where those designations appear in this book, and Addison-Wesley was aware of a trademark claim, the designations have been printed in initial capital letters or all capital letters.

The author and publisher have taken care in preparation of this book, but make no expressed or implied warranty of any kind and assume no responsibility for errors or omissions. No liability is assumed for incidental or consequential damages in connection with or arising out of the use of the information or programs contained herein.

Library of Congress Cataloging-in-Publication Data

Boone, Barry
    Java essentials for C and C++ programmers / Barry Boone.
        p.   cm.
    Includes index
    ISBN 0-201-47946-X
    1. Object-oriented programming (Computer science) 2. Java
(Computer program language) I. Title.
    QA76.64.B675 1996
    005.13'3—dc20   96-3973
                                                      CIP

Sponsoring Editor: Kim Fryer
Project Manager: John Fuller
Production Coordinator: Ellen Savett
Cover design: Jean Seal
Text design: Kim Arney
Set in 12-point Adobe Garamond by Pure Imaging

1 2 3 4 5 6 7 8 9 -MA- 0099989796
First printing, April 1996

Addison-Wesley books are available for bulk purchases by corporations, institutions, and other organizations. For more information please contact the Corporate, Government, and Special Sales Department at (800) 238-9682.

Find A-W Developers Press on the World-Wide Web at:
http://www.aw.com/devpress/

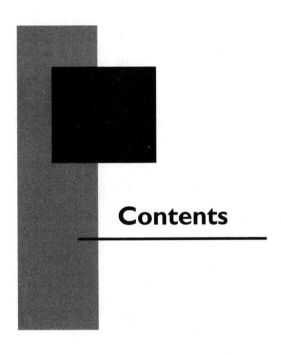

Contents

Acknowledgments

Thanks to Dylan McNamee for his enthusiastic support in helping ensure this book's accuracy and its coverage of the important topics. He conceived of and wrote the terrific TownHall and FileBrowser applications included in this book and contributed some of its deeper insights. Dylan is a graduate student at the University of Washington's computer science department with Geoff Voelker, another amazing Java dabbler. Geoff thought up and developed JavaWalker and JavaTalker, both great applications that show how Java programs can run seamlessly with the Internet.

Kim Fryer and Keith Wollman are wonderful partners at Addison-Wesley and really got this project rolling. Thanks for their confidence, inspiration, and support.

I'm grateful to Dan Shepherd for our many fun and lively discussions about the Internet and the Web and also to John Matheny for his early encouragement in taking on this project.

And, as always, thanks to Mary for helping me in more ways than I could ever say or even remember.

Introduction

Being on the leading edge of software development, you want to learn Java. Fast. You already know C and something of C++. What's the most efficient way to learn the language? One that will give you a secure foundation from which to create your own cool applications and explore the language in more detail? To start with, you can read this book!

■ WHAT'S HERE?

Java Essentials for C and C++ Programmers is a great way to understand Java from the point of view of what you already know. This book's streamlined approach is organized as follows:

Part I: Concepts: The early chapters show you the paradigm shifts you'll make when programming in Java rather than in C and C++.

Part II: Quick Start: The middle chapters provide a quick start for Java development; you'll learn the basics of Java's program structure, how to obtain input, and how to display output.

Part III: Details: The later chapters leverage what you already know about programming to teach you the language and give you the knowledge you need to fully understand the fine details.

■ IS THIS BOOK ANY FUN?

One of the aspects that's most fun about this book is the applications. In addition to a ton of code snippets, I've included a number of applications that not only show how the language and class libraries work but also are fun to run. You'll find a visual Web crawler called *JavaWalker,* an Internet chat program called *JavaTalker,* a swinging pendulum, a model of a town hall filled with feisty citizens, some calculations concerning time dilation if you happen to be traveling to Andromeda, and many more—all written in Java and fully explained here. You might be surprised to find how straightforward a number of these are and how easy Java makes writing these graphical multitasking applications.

■ WHY LEARN JAVA BY COMPARISON?

There is an inherent struggle between C/C++ and Java. Though they are similar in many ways, they were built with different worlds in mind. Being a C/C++ programmer to start with, you'll want to compare Java with its predecessors almost constantly while you're first learning this new language. This book doesn't flinch from the collision of these language powerhouses.

In some sense, you can think of this book as a superconducting supercollider. This book takes C/C++, positions it in a bubble chamber, and then hurls Java at it to record the shower of new particles, ideas, and insights that emerge. These will help you see the building blocks of these languages much more fully than you could by just analyzing one language in isolation.

And, perhaps most importantly, since this book is for programmers, *Java Essentials for C and C++ Programmers* gets right to the good stuff!

■ WHAT DOES THIS BOOK HAVE TO OFFER?

This book is intended to be used to first learn the Java language if you already know programming. Going further, since this book includes complete applications, you can also use it as a reference to explore the fine details of Java software development. If you know C and C++, this is the fastest, most efficient way you can learn the Java language. If you've already explored Java a little, this book also makes a great reference for clarifying concepts and relating your programming experience to this new language. *Java Essentials for C and C++ Programmers* bridges the gap between a knowledge of C and C++ and a mastery of Java.

In addition to learning Java, you'll gain a new perspective on modern computer languages. You'll see exactly where Java improves on C and C++ from an ease-of-programming point of view. You'll discover the elegance and the power of this new object-oriented language that is winning converts around the world and throughout the Web.

Good luck in your explorations! And, just like that, the future is now, and it's time to begin.

PART I

Concepts

The chapters in Part I offer an overview of Java programming concepts, relating them to your programming experience. These chapters define terms and use diagrams to help you see the power of Java. They also explain the approach to use when developing software with Java and compare this approach with developing in C and C++.

There's very little code in these first five chapters. If you're really eager to get started, you might want to jump ahead to the Quick Start section (Part II). The purpose of Part I is to provide a context in which to understand Java. You'll see quite quickly that there's more than just a different set of syntax and statements to understand. Java takes full advantage of new and more powerful ways to build software. Understand the next five chapters and half the battle is won. The rest of the language will follow easily from what you learn here.

Part I is organized as follows:

Chapter 1: The Philosophy of Java: This chapter introduces the themes that make up this book and previews the applications that will illustrate these themes.

Chapter 2: How Java Implements Object-Oriented Programming: This chapter provides a brief discussion of Java's object-oriented nature and compares Java's features with C++'s implementation of object-oriented programming.

Chapter 3: Language Foundations: Java manages many of the details of allocating and freeing memory, coordinating among competing processes, and signaling errors; this chapter introduces the ways in which Java provides a foundation for software development.

Chapter 4: Development Cycles: Developing in Java is subtly different than developing in C++; this chapter provides an overview of why this is so.

Chapter 5: Java Environments: Java can be used for stand-alone platforms as well as for distributed environments, such as the World-Wide Web; this chapter discusses the environments in which Java programs run.

By the time you're through with Part I, you'll have gained an excellent appreciation of what makes Java tick.

1

The Philosophy of Java

Chapter 1 uses the applications that appear throughout this book to illustrate some of the design ideas incorporated into Java. The applications featured in this book include a simulation of citizens up in arms, a few scientific explorations, a visual Web crawler, and an Internet chat program—to name just a few. This book is also filled with lots of working code snippets that illustrate points discussed along the way. By taking a brief tour of some of these applications, this chapter introduces you to the themes that will appear again and again as you progress through this book. These themes all relate to the fact that Java is *simple, familiar, object oriented,* and *innovative.*

■ SIMPLE

Okay, be honest. In your life as a C/C++ programmer, how many times have you referenced a pointer that pointed to garbage? Or how many times have you referenced elements beyond the end of your array? Or destroyed an object that you still referred to elsewhere in your program? Once? A few dozen times? You lost count?

Java is a simple language. You can't program at the same low level that you're used to doing in C and C++. For example, you can't point to arbitrary locations in memory. You don't have constructs such as templates, unions, and macros. There's no such thing as pointer arithmetic. So, then, can you do less with Java? No. You can do more. And you can do it faster.

The next few chapters will show you some of the assumptions you've made about programming and how C and C++ have shaped your world view. Old paradigms are hard to break, so bear with these few short Concepts chapters so that by the time you hit the Quick Start chapters of Part II and the Details of Part III you'll already see the world from Java's point of view.

One theme this book will return to is the tension between ultimate code speed and programmer flexibility versus ease of power programming. C and C++ take the first path; Java takes the latter.

For example, suppose you want to simulate a pendulum. You have a great many approaches you can pursue in C++. In fact, it's not long before you start thinking about the implementation details. When should you use objects or structures? When do you need to allocate and free memory, and how much? How should you handle errors? How will you pass values between your functions, and what pointers do you need?

To make matters even more complicated, you might want the pendulum to swing independently of the rest of the application. For example, what if you wanted to show two pendulums at once? What about three? Do you need to write code that keeps on switching between any number of pendulums, allotting system resources yourself as required by your pendulums?

You might also want your application to show an animation of the pendulum swinging back and forth, so you'd think about programming for a graphical environment such as Solaris, Windows, or the Mac. And, since the whole world is becoming connected, you might want people to access and run this simulation over the Web as part of your home page.

You could handle all these details yourself, but why bother? Java can handle the details for you. Instead of having multiple versions of the same source code (one for each target platform), handling all the multitasking and synchronization of events, dealing with memory in different operating environments, planning different graphical interfaces, and worrying about Web protocols, you could write a single Java application in a couple of pages of code and have it do everything you want it to do.

Figure 1.1   Pendulum running in Solaris

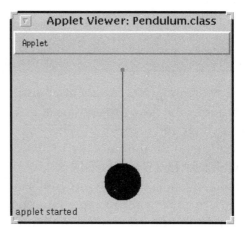

Your application might end up looking like Figure 1.1 when it runs in Solaris on a Sun SPARCstation.

What's more, your compiled program would run in Windows just fine—without modification. See Figure 1.2.

The chapters in Part III will explain how this program, Pendulum, is implemented. (Note that all of the programs not fully listed in the

Figure 1.2   Pendulum running in Windows

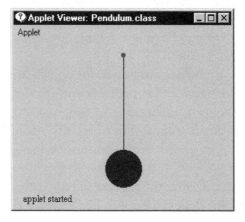

chapters themselves are presented in Appendix B. Appendix D contains other useful Web resources for this book.)

■ FAMILIAR

You'll find you can write programs in very little time because Java provides a familiarity for C and C++ programmers. Knowing C++, you'll also find that Java's syntax and many of its general principles are similar to what you're already used to. You just have to know how to match up what you know with how Java is put together.

For example, the quick start programs in Chapter 6 should feel quite familiar. These programs read simple input and display simple output, which is probably how you started out learning C and C++ in the first place. To help you along, the chapter first implements the C and C++ equivalents before showing you the Java version. That way, you can compare the behavior and syntax of some simple Java programs directly with the language that is already familiar to you.

■ OBJECT-ORIENTED

Depending on whom you talk to, object orientation is either the great savior of modern programming or a monumental waste of time. Part of the reason some people feel object oriented languages haven't fulfilled their promise is that even though a language (like C++) is object oriented, programmers lose many of the benefits they should gain from objects by squandering their time tracking down obscure bugs usually dealing with memory issues.

This is crazy. If you're going to write object-oriented programs, you should use a language that protects you from the ravages of the churning, bubbling, primordial soup of heaps, stacks, exceptions, and so on. It's very difficult to program only with objects when the language encourages you to directly access any arbitrary memory location (Figure 1.3).

Rather than wasting your time on bookkeeping chores, your thoughts should focus on your design (Figure 1.4). What are the objects in your system? What classes, instances, data, and behavior do you need?

Figure 1.3   Working with objects while managing the memory

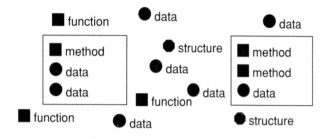

Figure 1.4   Only concerning yourself with objects

Java's object orientation makes prototyping a pleasure. We'll look at the steps that went into designing an application that crosses time and space and illustrates Einstein's special theory of relativity. The Einstein applet in this book illustrates the effects of traveling large distances at very high speeds (Figure 1.5).

Chapter 2 outlines how Java implements object-oriented concepts. For now, just repeat this mantra quietly to yourself: "There are only objects; there are only objects."

Figure 1.5   Einstein: the man, the myth, the applet?

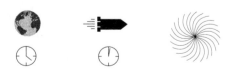

■ INNOVATIVE

Some very difficult or major problems in other languages and environments are not issues at all in Java. As Table 1.1 shows, by shifting the burden of supporting features such as memory management and synchronized multithreading from the programmer to the Java language and environment, the language becomes extremely powerful, and, by extension, so does the programmer.

For example, Java makes coordination among asynchronous threads part of the language itself. One of the applications in this book, Town-Hall, lets you listen in on a raging town hall meeting (Figure 1.6). Even though each of the five speakers in the town hall simulation is implemented as a separate process, and even though each speaker steps up to the podium without regard for the others and shouts out his or her thoughts, everyone gets heard and no one's opinion gets drowned out. This is possible because the application takes advantage of features built into the language to provide coordination among these independent speakers.

Another example of Java's innovation is its tight coupling with the Internet and the World-Wide Web. It used to be the play's the thing.

Table 1.1 Programmer and language responsibilities

Responsible Party	C/C++	Java
Programmer	Good, creatively written code Memory management Thread synchronization Platform specifics Error-handling protocols	Good, creatively written code
Language	Grammar and syntax	Grammar and syntax Memory management Thread synchronization Platform specifics Error-handling protocols

Figure 1.6 TownHall: listening in on outspoken citizens

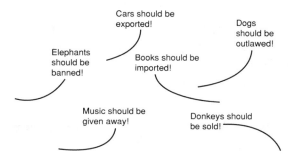

Now, the Web's the thing. All the world is an electronic stage. The Web isn't about to happen; it has already happened, and it's very likely you want your applications connected to this brave, new world.

One of the applications in this book allows you to interact closely with the Web to look beyond the immediate horizon of links. JavaWalker, a visual Web crawler, traverses links to allow you to look ahead any number of pages to see where the pages lead (Figure 1.7).

In addition to JavaWalker, there's also JavaTalker, a powerful, fun application that can be used to talk to other people on the Internet. You can use JavaTalker not only to learn about Internet programming but also to actually talk to your friends (Figure 1.8)!

Figure 1.7 JavaWalker: browsing beyond the immediate horizon

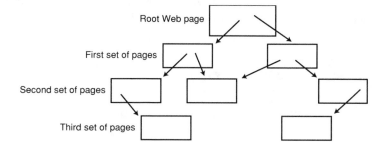

Figure 1.8   JavaTalker: chatting on the Internet

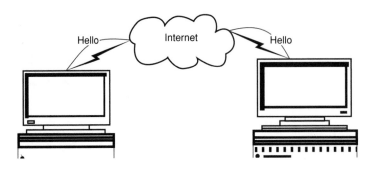

By looking at both of these applications, you'll learn a lot about Java's net package. The net package makes interacting with the Internet and Internet resources easy.

Another problem facing all developers these days is choosing a platform for which to develop. This is especially important when undertaking Internet programming, in which you can't determine which computers will access and try to run your software. You can choose based on sheer numbers of users, but even then environments change rapidly and you'll often find yourself updating your software each time there's a new operating system upgrade. What you need is an abstract windows toolkit.

For example, the Pendulum application mentioned earlier not only displays a swinging pendulum, it also allows you to interact with the pendulum itself, grab hold of it with the mouse, stretch its wire, change its initial angle, and let go to start it swinging again. As you'll see, you no longer have to concern yourself with the specifics of handling events in any particular platform; Java will take care of this for you.

▪ TYPES OF JAVA PROGRAMS

There are a number of programs in the Java constellation. These include

▪ stand-alone applications that provide a text-based user interface

- stand-alone applications that provide a graphical user interface
- applets that run in a Java-enabled environment, such as a Java-enabled Web browser
- extensions to Web pages written with a scripting language built on Java, called *JavaScript,* that tie together elements on a Web page
- protocol and content handlers that add themselves to Web browsers built with Java to extend the capabilities of the browser

This book's focus is on the first three items of this list. We'll explore Java's Web-specific aspects in Chapters 5 and 8. We'll return to the topic of the Web to fill in more details in Chapter 14.

■ SUMMARY

Java is a powerful language that simplifies the programmer's task. Java will feel familiar to C and C++ programmers, yet it takes over many of the responsibilities that used to be a programmer's job. This allows programmers to concentrate on the specifics of the application, rather than on its implementation on a particular platform. For example, by taking over the bookkeeping aspects of managing the memory, Java can provide an elegant object-oriented environment that will never leak memory or accidentally mangle it. Java's packages and its interpreted nature help you program in a platform-independent manner. You can develop multitasking programs by taking advantage of the features of the language itself. And, without your lifting a finger, the same source code you write on one platform can be run on just about any graphical environment connected to the World-Wide Web.

■ WHAT'S NEXT?

So now you know some of the key themes that will run through this book. Before you continue on, you need to understand how Java implements object-oriented programming. Then, with the right terminology under your belt, you can forge ahead.

2

How Java Implements
Object-Oriented Programming

Chapter 2 shows you (the C++ programmer) how Java implements object-oriented programming. This chapter explains how Java's approach is similar to what you already know from C++ in some cases and how it's different from what you're used to in others. In particular, this chapter covers how to use Java's classes, how to define data and behavior for your own classes, and how you might organize your class hierarchies. This chapter closes with a quick look at the differences between Java's and C++'s implementation of object-oriented concepts.

■ YOUR APPLICATION IS A COLLECTION OF CLASSES AND INSTANCES

C++ enables you to use objects. Objects are bundles of data and behavior, and, as the language's name implies, this feature puts it one-up on C. (I don't know how Java's name, in turn, relates to C++, except to quote from Sheikh Abd-al-Kadir, who said in the sixteenth century,

"No one can understand the truth until he drinks of coffee's frothy goodness.")

In C, you can create structures that group together related data. C++ enables you to define and create objects, but that's as far as the language and its libraries go. The C++ libraries, while sometimes using objects themselves (for example, the standard output is represented by an object), do not provide a collection of classes for you to build upon. That is, they do not provide a class framework. Though various third-party vendors do offer class frameworks, these frameworks are generally platform specific, while Java's class framework offers platform independence.

In Java, classes, in fact, provide the outlines for your applications. You can't define free-floating variables or functions. All behavior must belong to classes and instances, and all data must reside inside classes and instances. To run a Java program, you don't execute a file or call `main()` directly. Instead, you call the Java interpreter, passing it the name of the class. The Java interpreter, in turn, calls the class's `main()` method.

■ YOUR CLASSES AND INSTANCES CONTAIN DATA AND BEHAVIOR

You can't have globals or variables floating around in your application somewhere, unattached to a class or an instance, as you can in C++. In Java, all data and behavior must be part of a class or an instance.

There are special keywords you can use to specify whether your data or method belongs to a class or to each instance. You can also specify that your data or methods are `public` (accessible to anyone), `private` (accessible only to objects of that type), `protected` (accessible only to subclasses), or accessible only to other classes in the same package (which is the default).

You can also mark a variable or method as being unable to be changed by declaring it to be `final`. For example, if you'd like to create a global constant, you can specify that the variable belongs with a class (by using the keyword `static`), that it's `final`, and that it's `public`. In effect, you have defined a global constant—a value you can access from anywhere in your application but cannot change.

■ INHERITANCE AND INTERFACES ENABLE CLASS HIERARCHIES

Much of the power of an object-oriented language comes from inheritance. Classes inherit from other classes, which allows your system to grow over time and encourages your code to be reused.

C++ is notorious for allowing multiple inheritance. This is great in theory but it can be confusing in practice. For example, suppose you have a Prune class that inherits from both Plum and DriedFruit, just as a prune inherits these characteristics in real life. But, as shown in Figure 2.1, what if they both inherit from the Fruit class? Which way does the system traverse the inheritance chain when executing a method, and do you execute the same method twice when you get to the top level by two different routes?

C++ has rules and guidelines for handling this situation. But admit it: It's complicated. It can lead to behavior you didn't intend.

As with most things, Java strives to eliminate programming errors such as unintended runtime behavior. Java avoids the difficulties of multiple inheritance while still allowing classes to share characteristics. It does this through the use of *interfaces*.

Interfaces are Java's way of sharing an API (Application Programming Interface) among different classes. Interfaces are not as powerful as multiple inheritance, but they do allow you to sprinkle the same design ideas among your classes, even when they're not related in the class hierarchy. Classes that take advantage of interfaces must fully implement any methods the interface defines, or they must be defined as abstract. See Figure 2.2.

Figure 2.1   Sharing full class definitions in C++

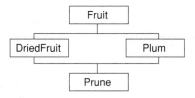

Figure 2.2   Sharing only characteristics in Java

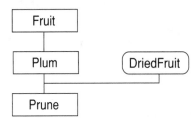

■ JAVA'S CLASSES ARE THE BASE CLASSES

In C++, if you don't explicitly state which class you inherit from, you don't inherit from anything (Figure 2.3).

In Java, if you don't explicitly specify an ancestor, you inherit from Java's system class Object. Just like a foal that can run with the horses as soon as it is born, so, too, do your own objects start life with lots of abilities since all classes inherit from an existing class (Figure 2.4).

Figure 2.3   C++: where your classes are the base classes

Figure 2.4   Java: where Java's classes are the base classes

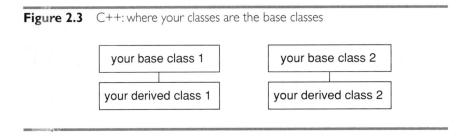

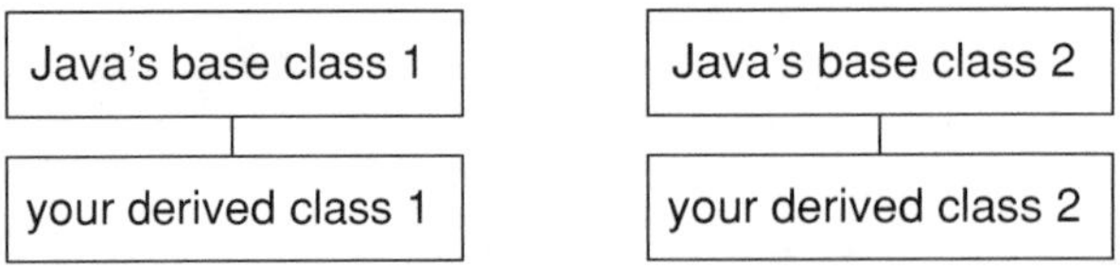

Since all functionality belongs to classes and instances, Java's packages (the equivalent of the C/C++'s system libraries) could not simply be a collection of functions that you use to interact with the system (as they are in C/C++). Rather, Java's packages are collections of useful classes and objects. In addition to class Object, you can also inherit from any of the classes that come with Java's packages.

To override a method, you just write your own substitution method and put it in place in your class. You can call your ancestor's method by using the variable `super`, and, as in C++, there's also a `this` variable that refers to the object responding to a method call.

■ JUST HOW OBJECT-ORIENTED IS IT?

Let's cut to the chase: Just how far does Java's object-oriented nature extend? Are numbers objects? Can you make the assignment operator (=) do something cool and different? This section provides some answers to these burning questions.

Primitives

For speed and clarity, integers, floating-point values, characters, and Booleans are not first-class objects.

Wrappers

Now, that said, Java does provide classes that encapsulate the primitive data types. Instances of these classes not only maintain a specific value but also can convert to other values, including character strings.

Arrays and Strings

Arrays and strings are full-fledged, first-class objects. This can save you from most of the classic errors that some C programmers make. For example, you can't ever "fall off the end of the earth" and start referencing memory beyond the end of your array.

Operator Overloading

You cannot overload operators. While this can save you from inadvertently writing code that is totally unreadable, the lack of operator overloading can also stop you from implementing some powerful solutions that rely on this feature.

The Java language itself recognizes this limitation to some extent and does implement one exception to this rule: It defines another meaning for the plus operator (+). When used with String objects, + concatenates characters to produce a new String.

Method Overloading

You can overload methods. Like C++, Java can distinguish which method to execute by the parameter count and the parameter types.

Constructors and Destructors

Just as you can in C++, you can write constructors in Java. However, you cannot write a destructor because Java manages the memory. You can still get into the act of assisting Java with cleaning up memory; you'll see how this is done later in this book.

■ SUMMARY

Compared with C++, Java implements a streamlined version of object-oriented paradigms. Since everything (except for simple data types) is an object in Java, you also gain some power that you did not have in C++. For example, arrays and strings are objects, and Java comes with a full set of base classes that you can use in your own applications.

■ WHAT'S NEXT?

Object-oriented programming is one aspect of Java. Another is Java's memory management model. The next chapter explains how Java takes care of memory and compares Java's approach with C++'s outlook.

3

Language Foundations

The concepts in Chapter 3 relate to what occurs on the stack and in the heap. One of the keys to understanding Java is realizing how the language removes you (the programmer) from being responsible for what's happening in memory. This is much different from C and C++, where you manage many of the details yourself.

While reading this chapter, keep in mind the theme that runs through much of Part I and the book in general: Java makes the programmer's life easier by freeing the programmer from "bookkeeping" responsibilities. The topics touched on in this chapter include what data elements are available to you for structuring memory, how Java manages the memory even when performing multitasking, how Java goes about cleaning up memory when necessary, and what Java does when it encounters errors.

This chapter is perhaps the most important one in this Concepts section. If you have a good grounding in the concepts discussed here, you might want to skim this information, but make sure you understand what this chapter is all about so that these concepts won't be fuzzy when we implement them in Parts II and III.

Table 3.1   Language building blocks

Building Block	C	C++	Java
Accessing memory	Pointers, addresses	Pointers, addresses, objects	Objects
Grouping data	Structures	Structures, classes	Classes
Defining behavior	Functions	Functions, methods	Methods

■ BUILDING BLOCKS

Table 3.1 provides a sense of how much simpler Java is than C and C++.

This table points out that C++ has evolved from C by adding object-oriented elements. However, C++ still retains the ability to subvert object-oriented programming by directly accessing memory. Java breaks the connection with C's "you manage the memory" mentality, retaining only C++'s object-oriented pieces.

This simplicity can be one of the most difficult things to grasp. Java lets you—nay, forces you to—concentrate on your application, not on managing the memory, coordinating between the interface and implementation, keeping track of the bounds of arrays, and so on.

■ EXECUTION

There are lots of analogies for invoking a program. These include running a machine, watching a stage performance, and simulating the world around us. But no matter what analogy you choose, none of them have the concept that only one thing occurs at a time. Why should your program be tied up in a straightjacket when most modern operating environments allow multitasking? Let your program loose in the fun house! Here's what it's all about.

What Is a Thread?

Before we look at what it means to have multiple threads, let's make sure we understand single threads. Threads are a good visual image: You might imagine a spool of thread unwinding or a trail of thread meandering across a table. No matter what twists and turns the thread takes, it's still sequential. An individual thread has a beginning and an end, and it never breaks into two strands or has gaps in the middle.

By *threads*, we mean threads of control or instruction sequences. Threads of control can be looked at from four perspectives: what the user sees, what the programmer sees, what the operating environment sees, and what the hardware sees.

From the user's point of view, a single thread of control is simple to follow. The user pursues a path that leads from launching the program, maybe entering input, viewing results, and then halting the program. If the user asks the program to download something from the Web, a program with only a single thread of control would stop whatever else it was doing to undertake the download because it would be able to concentrate on only one thing at a time. While users tolerate such behavior, it's only with a heavy sigh.

From the programmer's perspective, implementing a single thread is the classic top-down approach to software design, which C promotes. A program starts with some initialization, performs its calculations, displays any results, and then ends. See the example in Figure 3.1.

Figure 3.1   Top-down design: an example of implementing a single thread

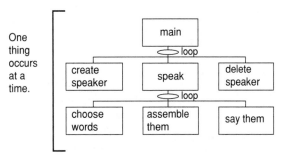

As far as the operating environment is concerned, all of its attention is devoted to one task at a time. The operating environment need only concern itself with a single stack. It's a no-brainer for the operating environment: It simply supports the program as the program does its thing.

From the hardware's point of view, if there's only one CPU, only one thing can ever truly occur at once. On machines where there is more than one processor, this is not necessarily the case. However, with the right programming language, it's easier to take full advantage of the power these machines have to offer.

Multiple Threads

For multiple threads, there are simply multiple spools. Each thread still follows one path; there are just many of them, all meandering across your table.

For instance, the town hall application in this book puts a number of speakers into action at once. Each speaker is independent of the others and is programmed as its own thread. Each speaker has a life of its own and runs sequentially. Taken together, there are multiple events occurring at the same time, as the example in Figure 3.2 shows.

Figure 3.2   A Java application where multiple things occur at once

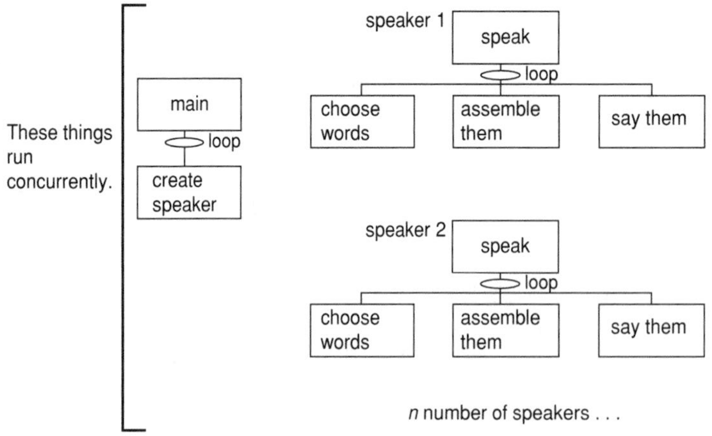

From the user's point of view, multiple threads imply that there is more than one thing occurring "at the same time." From the programmer's perspective, classes naturally lead you to thinking about multiple threads. Once you've divided your application into a bunch of independent (and perhaps collaborating) classes, why should all instances except for one have to go into hibernation? Why should there even be a concept of "only one thing at a time" at all, when each class is a bundle of behavior with clear boundaries to separate each one from all the other classes?

Classes and speakers aside, there are many situations where it's only natural to have multiple events occurring at the same time. Such applications range from complex business and engineering simulations to realistic animation to arcade games. So how can you simulate "real life" using your computer?

C and C++ Expect Single Threads

Unfortunately, for a C++ programmer, implementing multiple threads involves lots of bookkeeping. This is necessary because C and C++ were not created with multiple threads in mind. The bookkeeping you'd be required to perform includes coordinating among threads, scheduling threads, and determining when to start and stop a particular thread. As with class frameworks, although some third-party vendors do offer thread libraries, these are again platform specific, while Java's threads are platform independent.

Java Expects Multiple Threads

Fortunately, for a Java programmer, implementing multiple threads means taking advantage of the language and class libraries. Java itself handles the coordination and scheduling of threads.

Here's an example. The operating environment needs a way to keep track of multiple threads of control, so Java manages a separate stack and registers for its threads. Objects, however, coexist in the heap. If threads are running independently of one another, how can you stop one thread from updating data while another thread is right in the middle of its own update? The classic example is the updating of a bank balance. Suppose you and your spouse are using different teller machines to access your joint savings account. You are depositing $50, your spouse is withdrawing $50, and your current balance happens to be $50.

You start your transaction. The teller machine accesses your joint savings account and retrieves the $50 balance. At this point, your spouse accesses the joint savings account and retrieves the bank balance as well. The balance for your spouse also reads $50, which, as of this moment, is correct.

You complete your deposit. Your transaction updates the joint savings account balance that it knows about by adding $50 to it and sets your account to $100. Then, your spouse's transaction completes, subtracts $50 from the balance it knows about, and places the result of $0 into your account information.

You can stop this kind of disaster from occurring by coordinating when shared data can be modified (Figure 3.3). You'll learn all about synchronization in Chapter 11.

Chances are the computer on which your software is executing has a limitation of one instruction per CPU clock tick. So how can more than one thread execute at the same time?

The Java runtime environment chooses which thread gets access to the CPU. It does this by scheduling events based on priorities. All threads are *not* created equal: The thread with the highest priority wins.

If there's more than one thread with the highest priority, the Java runtime alternates between them, or all three of them, or however many there are (Figure 3.4).

Figure 3.3   Coordinating asynchronous threads

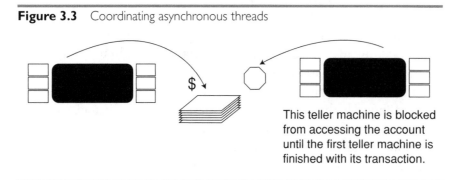

This teller machine is blocked from accessing the account until the first teller machine is finished with its transaction.

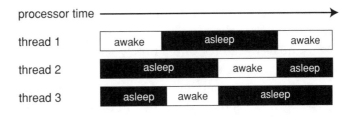

Figure 3.4 Switching between threads with the same priorities

■ MEMORY

Continuing its theme of making the programmer's life easier, Java also takes over responsibility for the heap.

Memory Is Your Responsibility in C and C++

C and C++ are geared toward allowing programmers to write tight, efficient, flexible code. One of the ways C delivers on this potential is by allowing you to allocate memory when you need it and free it when you are through using it.

You can do similar things in C++. You can allocate the memory for a new object, which grabs a chunk of memory from the heap. When you're through with the object, you can recycle the memory by returning it to the heap.

In addition, you can reference memory by obtaining the address of any variable to which you have access. By using an address, you can perform all sorts of extremely flexible pointer arithmetic.

While all of this is very powerful, it's also very dangerous. In particular, three logic errors can occur in your program that have, in fact, occurred in the code of tens of thousands of programmers since the inception of C:

1. Forgetting to ever free memory (resulting in a memory leak).
2. Freeing memory too soon (resulting in bad pointers).
3. Pointing to the wrong location in memory (corrupting variables or the stack).

The solution, of course, is to design, code, and test well enough to avoid these problems. Unfortunately, programmers are only human (at least, that's the way they are at the moment!), and a common feeling among programmers is that you can have only two of the following three elements: quality, features, and a timely schedule. If you want any two of these, you must give up the other one.

Let's say we accept a certain level of bugs in our software, which is the case today. Now let's look at the situation on the Web. You want to download and run applications inside Web browsers. If you continually encountered code that crashed (because of bad pointers), that mucked around with the memory in your machine (because you can access/replace any arbitrary memory location), or that occasionally went berserk and started filling up your system's memory (because of memory leaks), you'd soon come to hate the whole idea of executable content. Since these memory bugs are all related to the language, one solution is to change the language.

Memory Is the System's Responsibility in Java

One of the primary concerns you might have in changing languages is the possibility of losing the power inherent in your (native) language. I'm referring, of course, to possible fears about switching to Java, but fear not. You can still allocate and free memory. However, you will *never* encounter any of the three problems previously listed, nor will you ever have any other problem related to pointers, to addresses, or to allocating or freeing memory. The reason is that Java moves the memory management chores away from the programmer and takes them over for itself.

One of the mechanisms Java uses to do this is that of automatic garbage collection. Java's garbage collector is always running as an independent thread. If Java detects that an object is no longer needed, it zaps the object in question.

The specifications for the Java runtime do not explicitly state the algorithm for a garbage collection mechanism. Even so, it's still instructive to understand the concepts of garbage collection so that you can see what makes Java tick. One popular garbage collection algorithm is called *mark and sweep*. The idea behind this algorithm is as follows.

Figure 3.5 Mark (by following the links)...

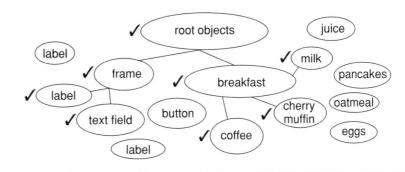

Start with a base set of objects. These might include globals, objects in the current stack frame, and objects within the Java runtime itself. The garbage collector starts by finding all the objects to which these base objects refer and then continues on by finding the objects to which these objects refer, and so on, until the garbage collector has followed all of the reference chains. The garbage collector marks the objects it finds as it sweeps through the object references. See Figure 3.5 and 3.6 for an example.

Since you can't cook up your own pointers, you can't obtain an arbitrary address, hang onto it, and try to use it again later. You only have objects. If you can still reference it from your application, the garbage collection routine will find out about this because it will encounter your object as it traverses the connections between objects. The

Figure 3.6 ...and sweep!

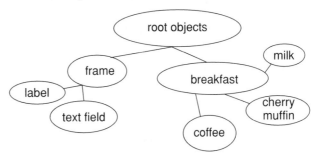

point is that you cannot pull an object out of thin air—you must have created it explicitly and retained a reference to it to be able to refer to it again.

After the garbage collector has gone through all the objects by finding the connections between them, it will go through the objects it knows are in memory. If any object has not been marked, it's a candidate for garbage collection because there is no way for you to get to this object ever again.

It's difficult to predict exactly when the memory will get recycled because the garbage collector continually runs as a low-priority thread. It doesn't really matter though. The object will go away only if you have no way to get to it anymore.

Note that you also can't flat out destroy an object. This could lead to the same problems with handling memory that Java helps you to avoid! For example, suppose you referred to an object in two places. If you deleted the object in one place, you might try to refer to it later from the other place. By relying on the garbage collector, you'll never have this problem. Once both references to the object vanish, the object will be gone for good.

Also, I can tell you from experience to trust the system. You might feel like you're being pulled blindfolded into traffic. Trust your guide. For example, suppose you define and create a new instance (therefore allocating memory from the heap). You assign this new object to a local variable. After a while, you don't need this object anymore. In fact, you need to assign a new object to the same local variable. Do you delete the unneeded object first? No way! You just do it—create the new object and assign it to the same variable. Let the original object just go away! You know the garbage collection approach: It's okay to put the peanuts on the barroom floor because the system will come along to sweep them up. Trust that you're not littering. You'll quickly see that it's all very liberating.

The main reason this approach is likely to upset you at first is that you'll feel as though you're not being very efficient. Again, C and C++ are tailored to speed, efficiency, and flexibility. Leaving used-up memory just lying around might strike you as inefficient, and in C/C++ it certainly would be! But this is Java, and it's Java's responsibility to take care of the heap. Let Java do its job.

■ ERROR HANDLING

Just as Java manages the heap, so it also manages the stack. This is especially true for error handling, such as when you need to unwind the stack back to the place where you can recover from an error. Java throws exceptions when it detects serious errors. Your own code can catch these exceptions if you want to handle the error yourself. If you don't do anything, the interpreter will halt the thread where the exception was thrown. (Note that this does not necessarily mean your application will come to an end. If you have multiple threads, only the thread that caused the error will halt. The rest of your threads, if there are any, will keep on running.)

Error Handling via Return Values

Conceptually, in C, the simplest way for a function to report errors is to return a value indicating success or failure. Even though it appears at first that this provides more than enough power, this model is extremely inflexible. In fact, we would immediately run into an organizational nightmare if there were a few functions in between the caller and the function that detected the error. The most immediate concern is that each function must return the error back to its caller until someone decides to handle it.

In C, it's also possible to place a bookmark in the stack, as it were, and then try to execute a particular piece of code. If an error occurs while this code is executing, you can ask the system to back up to where you placed the bookmark and switch to your error-handling code. You can do this in C with the `setjmp` and `longjmp` commands. `setjmp` records the stack's state in a buffer defined as `jmp_buf`. When your code detects an error, you can issue the `longjmp` command, which takes the `jmp_buf` variable and an error code as arguments. The only problem is that this is not *the* standard mechanism for reporting errors in C. In fact, there *is* no standard. This is, for better or for worse, part of C's flexibility.

Error Handling via Exceptions

C++ provides a wonderful convention for reporting and handling errors: exceptions. The idea is that you can, as with `setjmp/longjmp`, set a location in the stack before trying to execute a particular block of code. If you or the system throws an exception, the stack will unwind to where you set the bookmark and execute any error-handling code the system finds there.

In fact, throwing exceptions gives C++ a chance to perform yet another memory management task. If there are objects that were created and that live on the stack, C++ can call their destructor functions to get rid of them when the stack unwinds back to the bookmark.

Error Handling in Java

Java does not have this particular problem because its objects will all exist on the heap. But there are still many benefits to using exceptions. Among them is the clean separation between error detection and error handling.

For example, with Java's imported packages, and with reusable libraries and classes in general, it's often difficult for a particular method to know how to handle an error. What if there is a conversion error when translating a string to a double value? Is this a banking application, where you can't make any assumptions and must sound all sorts of bells and whistles to tell the computer operator that something went wrong? Should the program terminate? Or can you just recover by simply changing the value to 0? By separating error detection from error handling, your own code can work together with any class library to make the right thing happen for your application.

■ SUMMARY

This chapter introduced the concepts relating to Java's language foundations and memory management schemes. Your programming task is simple in Java because Java takes over responsibility for the heap. Since you can't turn any made-up integer into an address, you can't access arbitrary locations in memory. This means you must deal with objects, and only objects, as you implement your Java applications. In addition, Java takes over the chores for coordinating among multiple threads of control in a multitasking application. Java also standardizes error handling by throwing exceptions when something goes wrong.

■ WHAT'S NEXT?

Another way to view Java in relation to C and C++ is to understand what it's like to develop in these languages. The next chapter takes a look at the steps that make up the development cycle for a Java application and so prepares you to start your own application development.

4

Development Cycles

The whole development cycle is subtly different for Java than for C and C++. You still design your program, write your source code, compile, and execute it. If you want to create a stand-alone library containing published APIs, you can even do that in all three languages. But underlying each stage in this process, the details are quite different.

Chapter 4 starts out generally with a discussion of designing object-oriented software versus designing procedural programs. It then delves into the details of what's occurring when you compile and execute your Java programs. The concepts in this chapter have relevance to the way in which you organize your projects and approach your application's development. So, hang on as we tour the stages that make up Java's development cycle!

■ FIRST QUESTIONS

For some amount of time—whether it's five seconds or many months—you will design your software. Both ends of the spectrum—from designing until your application is fully determined to diving in and programming "by instinct"—can either work out well or lead to serious problems. The language in which you program should guide you in finding a good solution to the problem at hand. This section takes a quick peak into just how C, C++, and Java lead you down particular lines of thought.

C: How Do I Want to Do It?

The first question in most top-down languages, including C, is "How do I want to do it?" or "What is the algorithm?" This line of inquiry is great for relatively small programs, where you can grasp the flow through the program and the interactions of its pieces. If you can't see the whole picture at once, you're likely to run into trouble at some point if you haven't spent some time structuring your software. That is, your functions will grow, and you'll notice you've started to duplicate code and need to create utilities out of them, requiring you to retest your application. You'll add constants, you'll move data into header files, you'll add parameters to calling sequences, and so on. Lack of design can become a real headache.

C++ and Java: What Do I Want to Do?

The initial question in object-oriented languages is "What do I want to do?" or "What are the objects in my system?" This line of thought can slow you down for very simple programs. You have to decide on the objects first before you can turn to implementing their behavior. But, for anything much longer than Hello, World, it's a marvel how well objects encourage you to work things out correctly.

The difference between C++ and Java in this respect is that C++ still allows you to approach your software from the "how do I want to do it" point of view. That's flexible and, of course, not surprising since C++ is an extension of C. Java, however, does not share C++'s compatibility constraint. The Java language forces you to think in terms of objects. You don't have a choice, as you do in C++.

■ SOFTWARE ENGINEERING

Creating software is both a design problem and an engineering problem. Writing software can be a rewarding experience because it allows you to build, in effect, ethereal machines that can do some very creative things. But writing software is also an engineering problem because you're constantly dealing with trade-offs such as code speed, size, maintainability, and application features.

Designing Procedures in C and C++

In C, you start out thinking about your algorithm. Chances are you'll design using a top-down approach. That is, you'll break the problem into smaller pieces, each piece becoming more and more specialized until you actually write the code to get your application to do something.

Designing Objects in C++ and Java

One way to find the objects in your system is to think about what it is you want your system to do. What will happen? (You're not yet looking for the *how*, just the *what*.) Thinking about what parts of the system you have in real life will often lead directly to the objects in your system. Finding the relationships among your real-world objects will often determine your class hierarchy. Eventually, ideally, you end up with a system of objects that maintain their own state and have behavior you can execute. These objects will likely collaborate so that the application can do its thing. That is, with an object-oriented design, you end up with a hierarchy of common behavior at the top and more and more complex behavior extending each level.

■ COMPILING

Traditional compilers translate your source files into the specific instructions your target machine understands. This section looks at what this means for C/C++ and for Java.

C and C++ Machine Code (Machine Dependent)

C and C++ programs, built for speed and flexibility, are geared primarily for creating the most efficient machine code possible (Figure 4.1). Unfortunately, since your program is inevitably optimized to a particular chip

Figure 4.1   The C/C++ development cycle

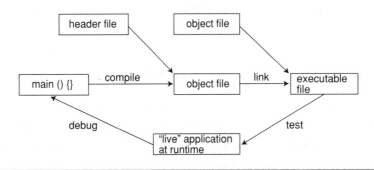

set, this creates machine dependence, requiring you to recompile your code for different chip architectures.

This topic has taken up entire chapters (dare I say books?) in C and C++ programming. It has occupied many people in standards committees, both on the language side and on the hardware side — and for good reason. We live in a heterogeneous world of computers. There are many different types of computers for many different purposes. Faster, more powerful chips with new instruction sets are constantly being developed. At the same time, programmers are finding new things they want to do and want the language to support.

Java Class Files and Byte Codes (Machine Independent)

Tailoring a program to a specific platform is desirable in stand-alone, homogeneous environments, and C/C++ allows you to write code that is superfast. However, the computer world is no longer a place of separate islands. The Internet in general and the World-Wide Web in particular are different landscapes altogether. By definition, the Internet is a network of networks, consisting of a variety of hardware and software platforms. The trick is that all these platforms speak the same protocol so that they can communicate seamlessly.

To add a programming element to the Internet that can permeate the Web, you cannot use C or C++ programs. First, there's the problem of security (Chapter 5 looks at some of these issues). Second, and most importantly for our purposes, a C/C++ program compiled for a Sun

SPARCstation will not, for instance, run on a Mac or in Windows, nor, for example, will a Mac program run on Solaris. What we need, especially for the Web, is an interpreted language. And, since we're all used to the power of languages such as C and C++, an Internet programming language should be powerful—something more than just a scripting language.

Powerful, interpreted languages can be slow, however. If the interpreter must parse the source each time it executes, our applications will move at a snail's pace.

Java overcomes this particular problem by compiling its source code into a machine language, though not one specific to any particular chip. The result of a Java compilation is not object code but *byte code*. The compilation result is basically a stream of bytes consisting of opcodes and parameters for a theoretical machine. This theoretical machine is called, naturally enough, the *Java Virtual Machine* (JVM).

The JVM can be embodied in any representation that suits your needs. When it is implemented in software the JVM stands between your particular machine and the Java programs you'd like to run (Figure 4.2). The JVM interprets the compiled Java source to run your application.

Compiling into byte code solves much of the speed issue. Unless Java runs on a chip supporting the opcodes of the JVM, native C/C++ code

Figure 4.2 The Java Virtual Machine

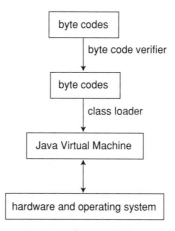

will almost certainly be faster. As this chapter emphasizes, the C/C++ and Java languages are geared toward solving different problems. For Java, the issues are simplicity, familiarity, object orientation, and innovation. For C/C++, the issues are speed, power, and programmer flexibility.

Java source code files identify themselves by the extension `.java`. The file that results from compiling a Java class is a byte-code file, identified by the extension `.class`. Even if you have combined many Java class descriptions in the same source file, the Java compiler will still emit a different `.class` file for each of your classes. When the JVM runs, it looks for any classes referenced by the class you're executing and loads these as well (Figure 4.3). Java, then, is also a dynamic language, not requiring that everything be defined statically at compile time; the JVM can link in the required classes on the fly.

It's often convenient to define one class per file. One implication of what has been said here is that there are no dependencies between source files during compilation. As long as your interfaces have not changed, there's no need to recompile various project files if an ancestor class or utility class, say, has changed. You need to recompile only the single `.java` file that's different.

So how are these byte codes arranged? When the JVM tries to use a class, it overlays the class file with a predefined structure. This structure has elements in it that can be of variable length. The structure contains fields that identify the class's class and superclass. It also maintains the characteristics of its fields, methods, and attributes (that is, whether they're `private`, `final`, and so on).

The first two bytes of the class file identify it as a class file. These two bytes spell out `CAFEBABE` in hex (I'm not making this up). The

Figure 4.3   The Java development cycle

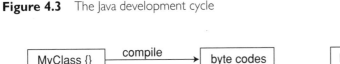
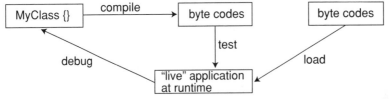

variable-length arrays in the structure are used to contain the information for fields and methods. The methods consist of opcodes generated by the compiler. These opcodes conform to the instructions understandable by the JVM.

■ RUNNING

Different things occur when you run a Java program than when you run a C/C++ program.

Executing a C/C++ Program

When you execute a C/C++ file, the system finds its way to your `main()` routine to get the ball rolling. The application runs until the `main()` function exits.

You might use dynamic libraries that you link in when needed, but otherwise everything is defined up front, linked in at compile time. Since everything is determined before you execute, you even know how the memory will be laid out for your application.

Interpreting a Java Program

When you execute a Java application, you specify the class you'd like to run. The Java interpreter starts at that class's `main()` method. This Java class communicates with other Java classes, as it desires. The JVM loads these classes as necessary.

Your application runs until the `main()` method exits *and* there are no more programmer created threads running in the JVM. So, for example, if you create and display a window in your class's `main()` routine and then your `main()` routine exits, your application will continue to run because the window will have a thread associated with it while it waits for input events. The application will continue to run until the user quits the window (that is, as long as no new threads were started).

Interpreting a Java program means that most details are determined at runtime, not compile time. In particular, memory is laid out at runtime and classes are loaded dynamically as needed.

■ ORGANIZING YOUR PROJECTS

In keeping with the theme of Part I, the Java development environment also takes on the burden of publishing your classes' APIs for use by other programmers (and even for use by yourself). This section describes Java features you can use to organize your Java projects with a minimal amount of work while still providing documentation and easy maintenance.

C and C++ Source and Header Files

In C and C++, you can define your interface in header files, which allows you to share classes and code among different files.

In theory, it's nice to think of your API as separate from its implementation. However, in practice, it's not always good to define the interface and implementation in two different places. This can lead to more work (and more errors!) in trying to manage and maintain duplicate information. Once again, you are doing the bookkeeping of maintaining your application.

Java Source Files

In Java, you can still think of your interface as separate from your implementation, but you don't define them in two different places. Your Java source files contain only one thing: descriptions of your classes. Unlike C++, you do not separate the declaration of your interface from its implementation. For example, in Java, you don't forward-declare your methods; instead, you define them in place. (We'll get to publishing your APIs in a moment.)

Packages

One way to organize your classes is by grouping them together into *packages*. Packages are similar to the libraries found in C and C++. You can think of packages as subsystems. Java comes with a number of useful packages, and Chapter 13 covers these packages in detail. However, you can also create your own packages to help organize your own applications by grouping together related classes.

To assign a particular class to a package, simply indicate at the beginning of your Java source file the package this class belongs to:

```
package maps;
```

You can assign any classes you'd like to any package. Simply put this line at the beginning of each Java source file where you've defined the class or classes you'd like to include with a particular package. Be sure to place the resulting `.class` file into a directory that matches the name of your package (in this case, into a directory called `maps`).

If you want another class to use a class that you've put into a package, you must first import the class. You can import all the classes in a package if you'd like to by using a wild-card symbol (*), or you can import only a particular class.

For example, to import all the classes in the `maps` package, you can write

```
import maps.*;
```

To import only a particular class, perhaps the details of a map called `Iceland`, you can write

```
import maps.Iceland;
```

Publishing APIs

Since Java keeps the documentation, interface, and implementation together in one location, the Java development environment comes with a handy tool for automatically generating pretty documentation of your classes' APIs in HTML (Hypertext Markup Language) format. This allows you to publish your APIs, for yourself and for others, without spending time managing separate header or documentation files. Instead, you just ask Java to construct these documentation files automatically, and off it goes.

With this documentation tool, you can still distribute your compiled classes and hide their implementations. Java includes the appropriate code comments by finding the comments inside the identifiers /** and */, as in

```
/** These comments appear in the HTML documentation
    * generated automatically. These comments should
    * only appear before declarations of classes, methods
    * and class and instance variables.
    */
```

■ SUMMARY

This chapter provided information about the Java development cycle. It contrasted Java development with C/C++ development and discussed running your application in both environments. In addition, the Java Developer's Kit (JDK) provides a tool for documenting your classes so that you can provide information about your classes' APIs separately from their source code.

■ WHAT'S NEXT?

The final chapter in Part I explores the nature of developing and running Java applets on the World-Wide Web.

5

Java Environments

Java can be compiled and run in any operating environment where an interpreter exists for it. Now, what happens if we integrate a Java interpreter with a Web browser? Ah, you've just asked the $64,000 question. The billion-dollar answer is that you transform the Web. In this context, Chapter 5 provides a quick look at why Java is perfect for the Web, introduces the idea of an applet, and provides an overview for what makes a Java-enabled Web browser different from traditional browsers.

■ TRANSFORMING THE WEB

Much of the attention surrounding Java concerns its ability to be downloaded over the Web and run on a client computer. Before Java, the Web was an amazing resource of documents, but they were only documents. Sure, they were hyperlinked, and that created a knowledge space much more powerful than if the same documents were collected as printed material in some huge book somewhere.

Primarily, this added value comes in the form of added information. Where before a document might consist purely of data, now linking two pieces of related data transforms the raw data into information. For example, exploring a page with pictures of a comet hitting a large, gaseous planet might include a link to an overview of the Solar System. Linking two pieces of information could perhaps lead to serendipity!

Java transforms the information itself. Rather than displaying a chart of data, a Java-enabled browser allows you to manipulate this information, run regression analyses, graph different points, change the scales, and so on. While you could theoretically do all this before by interacting with the server directly, the time required to pass the information back and forth over the network (the Internet) made the experience qualitatively different. Passing the document back and forth over a network still puts the end user in the mindset of working with a static document. The interaction seems more like requesting a different document than working with the one you have which, in fact, is exactly the situation. Working locally on your machine allows you to explore and manipulate the information in the document now directly under your control.

■   WHY JAVA FOR THE WEB?

Why do you need Java to write a program for the Web? What's wrong with C or C++? This section provides some answers.

Platform-Independent

First of all, running programs over the Web virtually requires platform independence. The World-Wide Web is open to anyone through a standard protocol that any platform can access. Applications on the Web should ideally blend right into this platform-independent paradigm.

Platform independence does not work well for programs compiled for a specific chip's instruction set. Instead, what you need is an interpreted language. An interpreted language fits in well with the Web, which is also inherently interpreted: Each browser interprets HTML commands as it feels is best to create a nicely formatted document.

While committees have helped standardize C and C++ to ensure that porting goes smoothly, C and C++ executables are specific to the instructions of the particular processor and API of an operating system. When you run a Java program, the JVM stands between your hardware and your application. The reason why this works so well on the Web is that Java interpreters are now part of the Web browsers themselves; when the browser downloads Java code, it hands it off to its interpreter to execute the program. Interpreting a "generically" compiled program such as Java byte-codes results in execution that's still quite fast while providing complete platform independence.

Secure

The Java interpreter ensures that you won't download any viruses. When a Java program is downloaded over the Web, it is placed in a restricted region of memory. The interpreter looks over all of the byte codes for the program and makes sure that they obey the laws and constraints of the language. If the byte codes are deemed safe, the interpreter lets the program run, but it still limits access to certain system resources.

Another aspect to the byte-code checker is that method invocations are stored in byte codes, not as addresses, but as names. In C/C++, these addresses cannot possibly be validated because C/C++ allows you to jump to any arbitrary address during program execution. In Java, only after the method names have all been determined to be valid are they resolved into specific locations in memory where the method resides.

Safe

The Java language also makes sure programs don't *accidentally* screw up memory. Arrays and strings, for example, are first-class objects and provide bounds checking. And, since there are no pointers or casting of objects into handles or addresses, you can't manipulate arbitrary locations in memory.

Multithreaded

The Web is inherently an environment in which multiple events are occurring at the same time. A language that is used for Web programming should make dealing with multiple events very easy. While users more or less accept that they are performing one task at a time on a stand-alone PC, using the multimedia-rich Web is a different matter altogether.

Java makes multithreading easy. It does so in two ways. First, Java provides classes that can execute as separate threads of control. Second, Java makes coordination among asynchronous threads part of the language itself, thus easing the programmer's burden.

Dynamic

The classes that make up an application do not need to be compiled into one giant executable. Rather, the Java runtime can determine whether a particular class it has just loaded requires another class and, if it does, can locate this class over the network and load it into the Java environment. In this way, Java applications can consist of classes that are distributed over networks.

Small

If the basic idea of Java applications existing on some central server and downloaded as needed is going to work, applications must be small. Home Internet users, for example, won't wait around forever while 10-megabyte applications are downloaded over 14.4K-baud modems. Java programs can be small because they leverage off of Java's class libraries and predefined packages. (You'll notice the applications in Appendix B are all quite small, even though they're packed with power.)

Standard

While C and C++ are standard languages that are well defined, different compilers generate different results. For example, some compilers insist you must return a value from `main()`; some use memory differently, assigning a different number of bytes to `int` values, which can affect the behavior of your code if you're performing math operations.

Java is already a de facto standard, with one implementation. The language specifications clearly spell out the memory requirements for its data types, the return types for its methods, and so on.

■ A NEW KIND OF WEB BROWSER

A Java application that runs inside a Web browser is called an *applet*. By using special tags in your HTML document, you can include applets as part of your Web page. Web browsers treat applets just like any other media element; the rest of the page flows around the space required by the applet (Figure 5.1).

Once a Java-enabled Web browser downloads the applet from the server, the applet runs on the end user's computer. Since applets are created using Java, they can range from simple animation to educational software, from games to business solutions.

Browsers built from Java, such as JavaSoft's HotJava browser, provide a way to extend the functionality of the browser itself. Java-built browsers can do this through the use of protocol handlers.

Figure 5.1   An applet as a Web page element

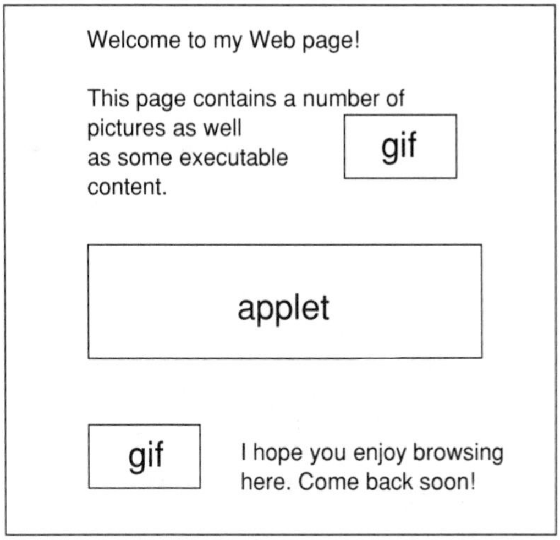

Welcome to my Web page!

This page contains a number of pictures as well as some executable content.

gif

applet

gif

I hope you enjoy browsing here. Come back soon!

A traditional Web browser (Figure 5.2) must grow in size indefinitely, incorporating each new protocol or content format that's invented, just to stay current.

For example, imagine the URL (Universal Resource Locator)

```
neigh://bluehorse.com/gallop.zqz
```

Even though your browser knows standard Web protocols such as `http`, it might not know how to handle the `neigh` protocol.

A Java-built browser (Figure 5.3) can seek out a new protocol handler when it encounters a new tag on a Web page that it doesn't understand. As each protocol is added to the browser, the browser gains in intelligence. It can, in fact, continue to gain intelligence forever, without the user ever needing to upgrade just to be able to keep up with developments on the Web. Or, put another way, a Java-built Web browser has the smarts to constantly upgrade on its own.

In addition to extending the protocols that a browser can understand, Java can also allow browsers to display MIME-encoded documents (Multipurpose Internet Mail Extensions) that they are unable to translate otherwise. In the preceding example, there's a file with the extension `.zqz`. While your browser might understand `.html`, it might not know about `.zqz`. Just as with protocol handlers, content handlers can add themselves to Java-built Web browsers to extend their functionality and usefulness.

Figure 5.2 A traditional Web browsers

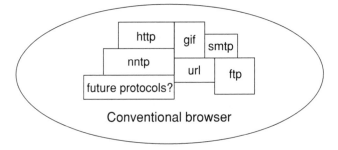

Figure 5.3 A Java-built Web browser

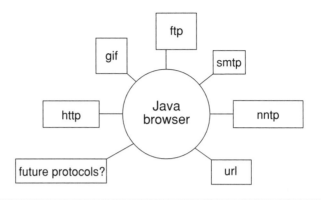

■ SUMMARY

This chapter provided a quick look at the context in which you're likely to run your Java application. You have the support of a variety of powerful class libraries, and you have the ability to run your Java programs securely over the Web. Also, at this point, you have an appreciation for the concepts that make Java different from what came before it. You are gaining a sense for what makes Java such a simple and powerful language.

■ WHAT'S NEXT?

Congratulations! You've come to understand Java's concepts. Now it's time to do some real work! Part II provides a quick start into Java programming. After that, you'll be ready for the details.

PART II
Quick Start

Now that you've read over some of the basic philosophy and ideas behind Java, you're ready to dive right in! The chapters in Part II provide you with a quick introduction to writing Java applications. If we happen to touch on some features of the language you don't understand, don't worry; we'll start at the beginning when we turn to the Details in Part III.

Part II takes you through three different types of Java programs:

Chapter 6: Text-Based Applications: This chapter introduces stand-alone applications that provide a text-based user interface.

Chapter 7: Graphical Applications: In this chapter, after seeing how to perform command line input and output, we rewrite these applications, again as stand-alone applications, but this time providing a graphical user interface.

Chapter 8: Applets on the Web: To round out Part II, this chapter adapts the applications developed in the previous chapters and makes them suitable for the Web.

After you've worked through the three chapters in Part II, you'll be ready to examine the Java language in more detail in Part III. The seeds planted here will allow you to see the forest for the trees later.

Keep in mind that these three chapters are intended to provide an overview of what Java programming looks like. In particular, these chapters aim to teach you how to

- accept input from the user
- calculate a result
- display output to the user

Implementing these simple programs will also give you a feel for the Java development cycle.

For information on how to compile and run these programs on your specific platform, refer to Appendix A.

By the time you've read through Part II and its sample applications, you'll have gained enough momentum to be headed toward the moon!

6

Text-Based Applications

Chapter 6 introduces you to some simple, text-based applications. We'll return to these programs again in Chapters 7 and 8, where we'll rewrite these text-based programs as graphical applications and applets. The programs in this chapter teach you the basics you need to learn for any language, including how to

- communicate with the user by reading input and displaying output
- define and access data and behavior to calculate a result
- write, compile, and execute a program to become familiar with the Java development cycle

This chapter shows you how to use standard input and standard output. The great advantage in having these examples as part of your first programming chapter is that you can relate the Java programs shown here directly to their C and C++ counterparts. Chapters 7 and 8 are based on graphical user interfaces, so they don't have C or C++ examples that correspond directly.

■ HELLO, WORLD!

The Hello, World program isn't the standard in computer science for nothing! If you can get it running, you've mastered a number of basics, such as writing and compiling a program, executing it, and displaying output.

To review: In C, the basic design philosophy is built on defining functions. As a reminder, the standard Hello, World program written in C is given in Listing 6.1. You define a function called `main()`. The runtime environment executes your program's `main()` routine to kick off the program. `main()` then calls another function (in this example, a C library routine) called `printf()`. Functions, functions all the way.

Listing 6.1

```
#include <stdio.h>
main()
{
    printf("Hello, World\!n");
}
```

In C++, rather than `printf()`, you use the object `cout` to display data to the screen. While C++ *uses* classes, C++ programs do not require that classes form their basic skeletons. For example, check out Listing 6.2, where the basic framework is still a function.

Listing 6.2

```
#include <iostream.h>
main()
{
    cout << "Hello, World!";
}
```

Now for Java. Listing 6.3 is the Hello, World program written in Java, and Figure 6.1 shows what this program looks like running in Solaris.

Listing 6.3

```
class HelloWorld {
    static public void main(String args[]) {
        System.out.println("Hello, World!");
    }
}
```

Figure 6.1   Hello, World! running in Solaris

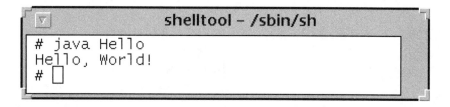

Not too radical-looking, you say? Even so, this little Java program illustrates some important concepts. Most importantly, you'll notice we've define a class, not a function, as the basic framework for the program. *Inside the class*, we've defined a method called `main()`.

Let's spend a few moments looking at the lowly Hello, World program so that you can gain a deeper appreciation for just what is happening here. What we uncover from this little example may convince you this program isn't so "lowly" after all!

main() and Arguments

Consider this line of code from Listing 6.3:

```
static public void main(String args[]) {
```

Now, what are all these keywords?

`static`—`static` methods and variables belong to the class that defines them. Here, the `static` keyword makes `main()` a class method.

`public`—Classes can control which objects are allowed to access their data and behavior. Making the `main()` method `public` means any object can access it from any package.

`void`—As you're familiar with from C++ (and as has been adopted by C), `void` means this method does not return a value.

You can pass arguments to the `main()` method using the parameters defined for `main()`. You'll also notice this is different from C or C++, where the command line parameters for `main()` look like this:

```
main(int argc, char *argv[]) {
```

In C and C++, `argc` contains the number of arguments passed to `main()`. `argv[]` is a pointer to an array that contains one character string per command line argument. The first parameter contains the name of the program that was invoked.

Java handles command line parameters differently. First of all, there's only one parameter, `String args[]`. However, unlike `argv` in the preceding C snippet, `args` in the Java program is not a pointer to anything—it is, instead, an array of objects. And, in Java, an array is also an object.

If you want to obtain the number of arguments passed to `main()` from the command line, you can get the length of the `args` array by accessing its `length` instance data, like this:

```
args.length;
```

(Notice that accessing data in objects is identical to how you do it in C++.)

Unlike in C, the number of command line parameters is not guaranteed to be at least 1. (In C, the first argument will always be the program name.) In Java, you're not executing a program per se—you're executing a class. You can always ask an object what its class is, so there's no need to pass this information along in the command line parameters.

Also, as already touched on in Part I, there are no pointers in Java. You can't accidentally "fall off the end" of an array and start accessing or modifying memory that's not part of the object you're dealing with, as you can do with the pointer `argv` in the previous C code snippet. If you try to access an element in the `args` array beyond its limit, you'll generate an `ArrayIndexOutOfBoundsException` at runtime. So, before you start grabbing command line argument, it's a good idea to check the length of the `args[]` array.

Packages

In C and C++, you must include `stdio` or `iostream` to be able to perform input and output. You'll notice there's no `#include` directive at the beginning of the Java program. How does Java get the system routines it needs to perform input and output?

Java includes a package called `java.lang` automatically. This package defines the basic object classes and performs standard input and output. To include other packages, use the `import` statement. Most of the example programs in this book use additional Java packages, so you'll see plenty of examples of how the `import` statement is used a little later on.

Executing Behavior

Java uses the same syntax as C++ to invoke a method:

```
result = instanceName.methodName(argument1, argument2, ...);
```

We invoked a method to write to the screen. We sent the string "Hello, World!" to the `println()` method for an instance of a Java class called `PrintStream`. The Java class System maintains this PrintStream instance in a class variable called `out`.

■ WRITING SIMPLE OUTPUT

We've said hello to the world. But which world were we talking to? What if we wanted to say hello to the moon? We'd need to know the earth's escape velocity—that is, the speed we'd have to be traveling vertically from the surface of the earth to escape earth's gravity and be on our way to the moon. Writing a text-based program to display this information illustrates the formatting of text and numbers and the defining of a variable.

In C, we have to hard-code how we want a number formatted (Listing 6.4).

Listing 6.4

```
#include <stdio.h>
main ()
{
   double velocity = 11.2;

   printf("The Earth's escape velocity is %4.1f kilometers per
second",
        velocity);
}
```

It's simpler in C++. All we need to do is tell the output device what we'd like to display, and it will format it for us (Listing 6.5).

Listing 6.5

```
#include <iostream.h>
main ()
{
   double velocity = 11.2;

   cout << "The Earth's escape velocity is "
        << velocity
        << " kilometers per second";
}
```

We do the same kind of thing in Java, calling a method and passing it the data to be displayed (Listing 6.6).

Listing 6.6

```
class Escape {
   public static void main (String args[]) {

        double velocity = 11.2;
        System.out.println("The Earth's escape velocity is "
                           + velocity
                           + " kilometers per second");
   }
}
```

All three of these programs provide the same output:

```
The Earth's escape velocity is 11.2 kilometers per second
```

So who said learning Java was rocket science? As the escape velocity program indicates, Java programs can be quite simple to understand.

■ READING SIMPLE INPUT

We know what we need to do to escape the earth's velocity. However, before we land on the moon, it might be good to know what we'll weigh when we arrive. Let's write a program that accepts our weight on earth, converts this to our weight on the moon, and displays the result.

The C Scale

We'll write the program in C first and build up quickly to an object-oriented Java program. Let's set up the program with the idea of future features in mind. That is, rather than just performing the simple conversion in a `main()` routine, we'll assume we're going to create records to maintain data for a variety of space travelers. Perhaps we'll later want to keep additional data for each astronaut, as well as calculate the astronauts' weights on other planets in the Solar System.

So, taking our anticipated future changes into account in our program's design, we'll define a structure to contain the astronauts' vital statistics. We'll also define a function to operate on the structure and calculate an astronaut's moon weight. This design will allow us to transition smoothly into an object-oriented C++ program.

Listing 6.7 shows what we can write in C.

Listing 6.7

```
#include <stdio.h>

typedef struct {
   int earthWeight;
} Astronaut;

double moon_weight(Astronaut *a)
{
  return a->earthWeight * .166;
}

main ()
{
   Astronaut astronaut;
   int       weight;

   printf("Enter your weight on Earth: \n");
   scanf("%ld", &weight);
```

```
    astronaut.earthWeight = weight;

    printf("Your weight on the moon is %6.1f",
        moon_weight(&astronaut));
}
```

Many subtle things are going on here, and, as an experienced C hacker, you probably know them all so well that you might just take them for granted. Here are some considerations.

Input is arriving as an address. What if it's not the kind of data you expected? The address doesn't care, but the declared data type certainly does!

Structures can be accessed and passed around in the program using pointers to memory. Though we're being careful about it, this is exactly where so many bugs creep into C programs. Using pointers to access (or to try to access) memory locations, whether or not you should be reading from or writing to these locations and whether or not these locations contain the data you think they do, has great potential for disaster!

The very large weight we've allowed (four digits to the left of the decimal point) is hard-coded. What if we change units of measurement? What if we want to see what our rocket ship will weigh? In C++ and Java, where the output objects (`cout` in C++ and `System.out` in Java) format the output itself, this isn't a problem. In C, however, it can be an important (and annoying!) design consideration.

In fact, none of these potential dragons raises its ugly head in Java.

A C++ Version

Now let's turn to a C++ version. In this case, you don't need to define separate structures and functions. You can combine the data and behavior into a single object. In the C++ example, we'll define a class called `Astronaut` (rather than a structure) that also knows how to initialize itself and calculate the astronaut's weight on the moon given its earth weight.

Our C++ version is shown in Listing 6.8.

Listing 6.8

```
#include <iostream.h>

class Astronaut {
   int earthWeight;

public:
   Astronaut(int wt) {
      earthWeight = wt;
   }

   double moonWeight() {
      return earthWeight * .166;
   }

};

main ()
{
   int    weight;

   cout << "Enter your weight on Earth: \n";
   cin >> weight;

   Astronaut armstrong(weight);

   cout << "Your weight on the moon is " << armstrong.moonWeight();
}
```

A Java Version

Two versions of this program are presented here. First, Listing 6.9 shows a Java version that most closely matches what we've seen in C++. Next, Listing 6.10, which appears later in the chapter, gives a version that separates out the user interface so that we can easily replace it later with graphical components.

Listing 6.9

```
class Astronaut {
    Double earthWeight;

    Astronaut (double weight) {
       earthWeight = new Double(weight);
    }

    public double moonWeight () {
       return earthWeight.doubleValue() * .166;
    }
}
```

```
class PlanetaryScale {
  Astronaut    armstrong;

  public static void main (String args[]) {
     char            c;
     double          earthWeight;
     StringBuffer    strng = new StringBuffer();
     double          moonWeight;
     Astronaut       armstrong;

     System.out.println("What is your weight on earth?");

     try {
       while ((c = (char)System.in.read()) != '\n')
         strng.append(c);

       earthWeight = Double.valueOf(strng.toString())
         .doubleValue();
     } catch (java.io.IOException e) {
       earthWeight = 0.0;
     }

     armstrong = new Astronaut(earthWeight);

     System.out.println("Your weight on the moon is " +
         armstrong.moonWeight());
  }

}
```

Figure 6.2 shows what this Java application looks like when it runs in Solaris.

Let's take a quick tour of this program and build on what you learned in Part I.

Classes

In the Java program of Listing 6.9 both the Astronaut class and the PlanetaryScale class are, by default, subclasses of Java's Object class.

Figure 6.2   PlanetaryScale running in Solaris

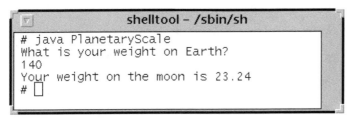

If we wanted to explicitly state which base class `Astronaut` inherited from, we'd write

```
class Astronaut extends Object
```

which is similar to saying, in C++,

```
class Astronaut : public Object
```

The major difference is, of course, that C++ does not define a base class called `Object` in the C++ libraries.

Instance Variables

In Java, by default, instance variables can be accessed only within the package where they're declared. Classes that do not specify a package explicitly using the `package` statement are considered to be in a package called `Default`.

Constructors and Other Methods

Java classes, like C++ classes, can define constructors to create and initialize new instances. Constructors in Java are similar in appearance to inline constructors in C++: They consist of the class name and a parameter list (if there is one), and they do not return a value. Constructor names are the same as the class name.

Other class and instance methods are defined very much like inline methods in C++. In Java, unlike in C++, you don't define a prototype for the method in the class definition and the actual method implementation elsewhere—the implementation is defined in place inside the class. (Remember, you only have classes. All method and instance definitions occur inside the framework of a class.)

Instances

Always use the `new` operator to create new objects. You can use `new` in C++, too, but you get back a *pointer to an object*, as in the following C++ snippet:

```
*armstrong = new Astronaut (earthWeight);
```

When you no longer need the memory for this object, you can purge it as follows:

```
delete armstrong;
```

In Java, memory management at this level is no longer your responsibility. Instead of a pointer, you get back an *object* from the new operator. First, declare the variable that will reference the object:

```
Astronaut armstrong;
```

Then, allocate and initialize the memory for the object:

```
armstrong = new Astronaut(earthWeight);
```

You can do both of these things in one step:

```
Astronaut armstrong = new Astronaut(earthWeight);
```

There's no need to ever explicitly destroy this object yourself, as outlined in Part I. Java handles reclaiming memory that has been allocated but has gone out of scope or is no longer referenced by any part of the system.

Data Types

One way to convert between data types is by using *wrappers.* Wrappers provide an object-oriented way of dealing with program data. For example, you'll notice that the variable earthWeight in Listing 6.9 is defined as a Double *object* (that's Double with a capital *D*), not as a simple data type such as double.

There are wrappers that provide object-oriented functionality for all of Java's simple data types. For example, the line of code

```
return earthWeight.doubleValue() * .166;
```

asks the Double object called earthWeight for the double value representing its data. (Wrappers can be very useful, so we'll return to the topic of wrappers in Part III.)

String and StringBuffer

Java maintains read-only characters using String objects. To edit characters, use StringBuffer objects. That is, once a String instance is defined, it can't be changed. StringBuffer objects, on the other hand, can always be added to and changed.

We use a StringBuffer object to read from the keyboard. One straightforward way to read from the keyboard that does not require special exception handling is to read one character at a time. In the Java application under consideration here, we use the StringBuffer method `appendChar()` to add characters to the StringBuffer object as they're entered, like this:

```
char    c;
StringBuffer  strng;

while ((c = (char)System.in.read()) != '\n')
      strng.appendChar(c);
```

Even when you're dealing with an instance that contains character data, when you use a StringBuffer, you must be aware of when to use a method that requires a String instead. To obtain a String instance from your StringBuffer instance, you can use a method called `toString()` to create a String using the StringBuffer's character data.

For example, the class method `valueOf()` that's defined by Double requires a String as input. So, using the preceding code snippet to read characters one at a time from the keyboard, we also use the method `toString()` to obtain a String from the StringBuffer:

```
earthWeight = Double.valueOf(strng.toString());
```

■ ANOTHER VERSION: ISOLATING THE USER INTERFACE

Okay, now let's check out the Java version that isolates the user interface. Since this version doesn't match precisely with the C and C++ versions shown earlier in this chapter, the simpler version was presented first so that you could compare the C, C++, and Java programs directly.

In Listing 6.10, the method `calculateWeight()` uses private methods to get the user input and display the output. In Chapter 7, we'll be able to replace the reading and writing of the data with graphical user interface components without changing the rest of the program.

Listing 6.10

```java
import java.io.DataInputStream;
   // to read a line from the keyboard

class Astronaut {
    Double earthWeight;
    Astronaut (double weight) {
       earthWeight = new Double(weight);
    }

    public double moonWeight () {
       return earthWeight.doubleValue() * .166;
    }
}


class PlanetaryScale {
   Astronaut    armstrong;

   /** Step onto the scale...
     */
   void calculateWeight() {
       armstrong = new Astronaut(getEarthWeight());
       showMoonWeight(armstrong.moonWeight());
   }

   /** Retrieve the value the user types in.
     * If the number was not typed in correctly, we
     * might get an exception. Be prepared to handle
     * this so that the program does not terminate.
     */
   double getEarthWeight() {
     double            earthWeight;
     DataInputStream   stream = new DataInputStream(System.in);
     String            strng;

     System.out.println("What is your weight on Earth?");
     // Try to read a line from the keyboard.
     try {
        strng = stream.readLine();
     } catch (java.io.IOException e) {
        strng = "0.0";
     }
```

```
        // Try to convert this value into a double data type.
        try {
           earthWeight = Double.valueOf(strng).doubleValue();
        } catch (java.lang.NumberFormatException e) {
           earthWeight = 0.0;
        }

        return earthWeight;
    }

  /** Display the result to the user.
     */
  void showMoonWeight(double wt) {;
      System.out.println("Your weight on the moon is " +
              String.valueOf(wt));
  }

  public static void main (String args[]) {
      PlanetaryScale ps = new PlanetaryScale();
      ps.calculateWeight();
  }

}
```

Program Structure

The idea here is simple. The main routine creates an instance of the class so that we can dispatch against it. We then ask the instance to calculate the astronaut's weight on the moon.

The method that calculates the weight retrieves the earth weight and displays the moon weight. Retrieving the earth weight involves asking the user to enter this value and then reading what the user enters. Displaying the moon weight involves writing to the standard output.

Error Handling

In this version, we've used an instance of a class defined in `java.io` called `DataInputStream` to read a line from the keyboard. This returns a String object containing the characters the user entered, not including the end-of-line character.

If something goes seriously amiss during our program's execution, the interpreter will throw an exception. If we haven't done anything special to anticipate such a condition, the program may come to a grinding halt.

Since `stream.readLine()` might throw an exception, we get
ready to catch it, as follows:

```
// Try to read a line from the keyboard.
try {
   strng = stream.readLine();
} catch (java.io.IOException e) {
   strng = "0.0";
}
```

Similarly, when we convert the string to a number, we must be prepared to handle an exception that signifies there was a problem with the
conversion:

```
// Try to convert this value into a double data type.
try {
    earthWeight = Double.valueOf(strng).doubleValue();
} catch (java.lang.NumberFormatException e) {
    earthWeight = 0.0;
}
```

■ COMMAND LINE INPUT

What if we wanted to provide our weight on earth as a command line
parameter? This chapter has already pointed out how command line parameters work and even how to check the length of an array, so let's put
that knowledge into action.

If this program required the user to input data via the command
line, we might provide a simple check near the top of the `main()`
method to stop the program if the user did not supply an argument. We
could write

```
if (args.length != 1) {
   System.out.println("Please include your weight on Earth as
                   a command line parameter.");
   return;
}
```

To access an element in an array, we can use standard C/C++ notation. For example, to retrieve the first element, we could write

```
args[0]
```

However, this element of the `args[]` array is a String instance, not a `double` data type. If we wanted the person's weight as a number, we'd have to perform a conversion. One way to do this is by asking a data type wrapper class to return a new object based on the value contained in the String. Here's an example:

```
Double earthWeight = Double.valueOf(args[0]);
```

To obtain a `double` data type from the Double instance, you can do what we did before: Ask the Double instance to return one using code that looks like this:

```
double wt = earthWeight.doubleValue();
```

■ SUMMARY

This chapter showed you how to create simple, text-based Java programs that you can execute from the command line. The basics covered here included

- obtaining user input
- displaying output
- defining classes, instances, methods, and data to implement your application

■ WHAT'S NEXT?

The next chapter takes the applications developed here and shows you how to add a graphical interface to them. Keep in mind these are still stand-alone applications that run independently of a Web browser.

7

Graphical Applications

Although most people associate graphical Java applications with the Web, these graphical applications can also run in stand-alone environments (that is, not within a Web browser). You can create your own window hierarchies and display them, or you can just use your applet with some minor modifications. Either way, as long as you have the Java Virtual Machine (JVM) running on your target platforms, there is nothing stopping you from developing any application using Java and distributing it with the Java runtime interpreter.

Even if you don't use the Web as a distribution method and a Web browser as a runtime environment for your applications, as you'll see here in Chapter 7, you gain three advantages over other approaches:

1. Your application will run without change on a wide variety of platforms.
2. You need to maintain only a single code base.
3. You can take advantage of Java's powerful graphics and networking libraries, multithreading, and object-oriented environment to create powerful applications quickly.

■ HELLO, WORLD!

Graphics Independence

One of the most time-saving aspects of writing applications for a variety of platforms is using Java's Abstract Windows Toolkit (AWT). This collection of classes enables platform-independent graphical user interfaces (GUIs). Without modification or even recompilation, the same classes execute in very different graphical environments and provide similar buttons, text fields, windows, and so on.

For example, consider a graphical Hello, World application. Figure 7.1 shows this is what it looks like running on a SPARC-based Solaris workstation, and Figure 7.2 shows the same application running in Windows 95.

Listing 7.1 shows the source code used in *both* environments. (Two debugging strings have been left in `main()`, which will be explained in just a moment.)

Figure 7.1   Graphical Hello, World! running in Solaris

Figure 7.2   Graphical Hello, World! running in Windows 95

Listing 7.1

```
/* This class says hello to the world using a graphical user
   interace */
import java.awt.Graphics;
import java.awt.Frame;

public class HelloFrame extends Frame {

   /** Without this the window name will say "Untitled". */
   HelloFrame(String s) {
      super(s);
   }

   /** Initialize the window size so that it appears nicely. */
   public void init() {
      resize(200,60);
   }

   /** Say hello to the rest of the world when we redraw. */
   public void paint(Graphics g) {
      g.drawString("Hello, world!", 60, 45);
   }

   /** This class method creates an instance of itself
    * and makes this window element appear. This is our
    * user interface.
    */
   public static void main(String args[]) {
      System.out.println("entering main...");
      HelloFrame f = new HelloFrame("HelloFrame");
      f.init();
      f.show();

      System.out.println("...leaving main.");
   }

}
```

An Overview of the Graphical Hello, World!

As with all Java applications, we develop a class, define its behavior, and then execute the class to get it to run its main() method. In this case, our class is called HelloFrame. Where before we extended (that is, sub-classed) class Object, now we're extending a user interface element called a Frame.

Four methods are defined in our new HelloFrame class:

1. `main()` creates and displays the user interface.
2. `HelloFrame()` is the constructor that allows us to define a title for this new Frame subclass.
3. `init()` sizes the Frame for this application (a Frame's default size is 0,0).
4. `paint()` displays our message within the HelloFrame instance.

We've also imported two classes from Java's window library that we used in the graphical HelloFrame application. The class Frame provides a top-level window for us to use for our application's display. The instance of class Graphics is passed to our `paint()` method when Java tells our user interface element (the HelloFrame instance) to redraw itself.

Window Hierarchies

You'll always find a Frame instance at the top level of the display hierarchy in a Java application. As you'll see in the next chapter, Web browsers can be the frame for a Java applet. For stand-alone Java applications, we have to create our own top-level frame.

The three important lines of code from Listing 7.1 are

```
HelloFrame f = new HelloFrame("HelloFrame");
f.init();
f.show();
```

These three lines of code accomplish the following:

1. Create an instance of our new Frame subclass.
2. Initialize the HelloFrame instance to its default size.
3. Show the HelloFrame instance.

This bootstraps our program, providing our own top-level window. In this case, the entire user interface consists of only this top-level window. Later in this chapter, we'll put other user interface components inside it.

The Java library called `java.awt` provides all of the user interface components you can use in your own applications. These graphical interface elements are abstracted from any particular implementation. The user interface elements in the AWT can be divided into two categories: those elements that provide the elements that users interact with directly (such as buttons, text fields, labels, pop-up choices, and so on) and those elements that are used to group and contain these buttons and text fields (such as windows).

In practice, you can think of the user interface elements as being either components (buttons, text fields, and so on) or containers (windows, frames, and so on). In actuality, class Container inherits from class Component, so, in a sense, there are only components. See Figure 7.3 for an illustration of the hierarchy.

main() Revisited

When you invoke the Java interpreter from the command line, it will execute your class's `main()` method and will run until the only threads left are the daemon threads. Creating and showing a Frame instance in `main()` starts another thread, even though `main()` ends.

To help you get a sense of this, some `println()` calls have been put in so that you can see this application continuing to run, even after `main()` has returned. As long as our HelloFrame instance continues to live, the JVM will keep on running, and our application will stay alive. When this user interface element goes away, our application will end if it has not started any additional threads of execution.

Figure 7.3   A partial class hierarchy for the AWT

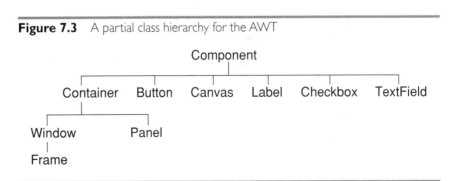

■ WRITING SIMPLE OUTPUT

Following our footsteps in the previous chapter, let's reimplement the application to display the earth's escape velocity. This time, we'll use a graphical user interface. As before, this application demonstrates that you can build up a text string by concatenating characters and other data types.

Listing 7.2 shows the Java source code. Again, we create an instance of the top-level frame in the class's `main()` method. Since we've created our own subclass of Frame, we can override the `paint()` method to display the string that we create out of the characters in quotes and the data value stored in `velocity`.

Listing 7.2

```java
/* This class displays the earth's escape velocity
 * using a graphical user interface.
 */
import java.awt.Graphics;
import java.awt.Frame;

public class EscapeFrame extends Frame {
   double velocity = 11.2;

   /** Pass the name of the window up the class hierarchy. */
   EscapeFrame(String s) {
      super(s);
   }

   /** Initialize the EscapeFrame instance. */
   public void init() {
      resize(300,60);
   }

   /** Display the earth's escape velocity when the
     * EscapeFrame instance redraws itself.
     */
   public void paint(Graphics g) {
      String string = "The Earth's escape velocity is " +
         velocity + " km/sec.";
      g.drawString(string, 30, 25);
   }

   /** Create an instance of this EscapeFrame class and show it. */
   public static void main(String args[]) {
      EscapeFrame esc = new EscapeFrame("EscapeFrame");
      esc.init();
      esc.show();
   }

}
```

■ READING SIMPLE INPUT

Now for the finale: a return to our earth/moon weight conversion program. This time, we aren't fooling around.

Since we designed the original, text-based version in a way that helped to isolate the user interface, we can now surgically remove the previous text-only UI and replace it with one based on AWT components and containers. Our new design approach involves

- using a text field for the user to enter the astronaut's earth weight
- displaying the moon weight within a window

Before looking at the source code, check out Figure 7.4 to see what the application looks like when it runs in Solaris.

Of course, being platform and graphics independent, the Java byte codes are interpreted by the JVM without modification on Windows 95, where the user interface looks nearly identical to the Solaris platform (see Figure 7.5). Even so, while the two interfaces are functionally identical, they are not necessarily *exactly* the same. Java's packages make an effort to use the look and feel of the target platform, so each platform's implementation uses the appropriate GUI guidelines.

Figure 7.4 Graphical PlanetaryScale running in Solaris

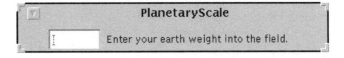

Figure 7.5 Graphical PlanetaryScale running in Windows 95

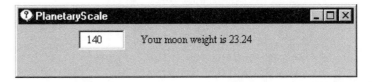

The Java source appears in Listing 7.3.

Listing 7.3

```
/* Displays an interface for calculating your weight on the moon.
 * PlanetaryScale - can be used as a basis for
 *       calculating your weight on a variety of planets
 *       throughout the solar system. In this version it
 *       simply calculates your weight on the moon.
 */
import java.awt.Event;
import java.awt.Frame;
import java.awt.Label;
import java.awt.Panel;
import java.awt.TextField;

public class PlanetaryScale extends Panel {
    Label        label;
    TextField    textField;
    Astronaut    armstrong;

    /** Step onto the scale... */
    void calculateWeight() {
        armstrong = new Astronaut(getEarthWeight());
        showMoonWeight(armstrong.moonWeight());
    }

    /** Retrieve the value in the text field.
      * If the number was not typed in as an acceptable double, we
      * might get an exception. Be prepared to handle this so that
      * the program does not terminate.
      */
    double getEarthWeight() {
      double wt;
      try {
          wt = Double.valueOf(textField.getText()).doubleValue();
      } catch (java.lang.NumberFormatException e) {
          wt = 0.0;
      }
      return wt;
    }

    /** Display the result to the user. */
    void showMoonWeight(double f) {;
        label.setText("Your moon weight is " +
                String.valueOf(f));
    }

    /** Set up the user interface. This consists of a text field
      * for the user to enter a value, and a label to be used to
```

```
 * display a result.
 */
public void init() {
    resize(400,60);
    // Make the text field 6 columns wide.
    textField = new TextField(6);
    add(textField);

    label = new Label("Enter your earth weight into the field.");
    add(label);

    armstrong = new Astronaut(0.0);
}

/** Respond to user actions. */
public boolean handleEvent(Event e) {
    if (e.target instanceof TextField && e.id ==
      Event.ACTION_EVENT) {
        calculateWeight();
        return true;
    }
    return false;
}

/** The class starts executing from here. */
public static void main(String args[]) {
  PlanetaryScale ps = new PlanetaryScale();
  ps.init();

  Frame f = new Frame("PlanetaryScale");
  f.resize(400,60);

  f.add("Center", ps);
  f.show();

  }
}
```

The PlanetaryScale class still collaborates with the exact same Astronaut class as before. Its code is repeated in Listing 7.4 for easy reference here.

Listing 7.4

```
/*
 * Astronaut - a class for storing
 *      information on different astronauts.
 */
class Astronaut {
    Double earthWeight;
```

```
/** Constructor */
Astronaut (double weight) {
   earthWeight = new Double(weight);
}

/** The astronaut can calculate its weight on the moon. */
public double moonWeight () {
   return earthWeight.doubleValue() * .166;
}
}
```

An Overview of the Graphical PlanetaryScale

You'll notice that the primary class in this application, `Planetary-Scale`, extends class Panel, while the other applications in this chapter extended class Frame. We need to use a Panel subclass here because we are now grouping more than one component into the container. Panels are an AWT class that you can use to arrange components and other containers.

Because we now extend a Panel rather than a Frame, the `main()` routine must be a few lines longer. We can't just display the Planetary-Scale (a Panel subclass) instance once it's instantiated: We still need a Frame instance at the top level. So, after creating the PlanetaryScale instance, we create the Frame instance, give the frame an initial size, add the PlanetaryScale instance to it, and show the frame.

Arranging User Interface Containers and Components

The graphical PlanetaryScale application arranges its user interface using containers and components. Figure 7.6 shows how the component hierarchy is put together.

Instead of simply displaying a frame that repaints with a particular message, the frame now contains a panel. The panel, in turn, contains a text field and a label. As you can discern from the source code in Listing 7.4 and from the picture of the user interface, the application uses the text field to allow the user to enter the astronaut's weight on earth and uses the label to display the astronaut's weight on the moon.

Component hierarchies can be arbitrarily complex. While it might be difficult to visualize the whole arrangement at once, keep in mind that each level is usually quite simple. At the lowest level, you can group

Figure 7.6   The component hierarchy for the graphical PlanetaryScale application

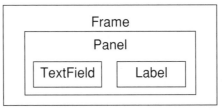

a few components together by using a panel. A few panels might be grouped together in another panel, and so on.

Some New Methods

The methods `calculateWeight()`, `getEarthWeight()`, and `show-MoonWeight()` also appeared in the text-based version in the previous chapter. Here, however, these methods work with the AWT components.

For example, the code fragment in `getEarthWeight()`

```
textField.getText()
```

creates and returns a String object representing the text in the text field.

To display the result, we simply set the text in the label:

```
label.setText("Your moon weight is " +
              String.valueOf(f));
```

The `init()` method was shown earlier in this chapter. Before, we used `init()` to set the container's size. Now, we also use it to create and add the user interface components to the container.

After creating each component, we use `add()` to add the component to the container. The container uses its layout manager to position the components according to your specifications. (You will find out more about layout managers in Part III.)

To understand `handleEvent()`, let's first look at how user events propagate through the window hierarchy.

Generating Events

When the user interacts with your user interface elements, the Java runtime sends events to the components or containers in which they occurred. There are a number of events your component might receive, including both keystrokes and mouse actions. As you'll see in Part III, the Pendulum application intercepts mouse events to track the mouse's position as it moves across the screen. As always, the Java classes allow you to work in a platform-independent manner, so you can track mouse movements in Windows using the same source code with which you track mouse movements on a Macintosh.

Handling Events

The Java runtime dispatches `handleEvent()` to notify a component that an event has occurred. For example, when the user hits the enter key after typing something into your text field, the text field will receive an event notification via `handleEvent()`.

If the text field itself does not handle this event, the text field returns `false` and the event gets passed up the component hierarchy. In the case of our application, the panel that contains the text field overrides `handleEvent()` and checks to see whether the event's target is in fact a TextField instance. If it is, then the panel handles the event and returns true, indicating we have handled this event:

```
public boolean handleEvent(Event e) {
    if (e.target instanceof TextField && e.id == Event.ACTION_EVENT) {
        // handle the event here...
        return true;
    }
    return false;
}
```

■ SUMMARY

This chapter showed you how to perform some simple input and output using Java's Abstract Windows Toolkit. The two key concepts to remember are as follows:

1. The user interacts with components, such as buttons, text fields, choice boxes, and so on. Containers group components in a hierarchy.
2. Events propagate up the component hierarchy until someone handles the event.

■ WHAT'S NEXT?

Now that you've been introduced to windows and events, the next chapter takes a quick look at how to incorporate these graphical applications into a Web page. You'll also see how you can make the same Java applet run without modification either in a Web browser or as a stand-alone application.

8

Applets on the Web

Applets sound like mini-applications, and they usually are. But they can also be full-blown spreadsheets, word processors, graphics studios, and the like. So what exactly is an applet? Applets are Java programs that can be run within a Web browser. However, as you'll see here in Chapter 8, you can also create Applet subclasses that know how to run as stand-alone applications, apart from the Web.

The Java runtime also invokes an applet's methods to help the applet run smoothly in a Web browser. This chapter works through the applications we've already seen to show you the changes you need to make to interact with a Web browser to paste these applications into the Web.

■ HELLO, WORLD! (AGAIN)

Executable Content

This, my friends, is the great promise of Java. Executable content is the sparkle on the Web page—it's the way to make the elephant dance. To start our exploration of applets, consider Listing 8.1, a Java applet that can be run as part of a Web page and greets the world.

Listing 8.1

```
/* This applet says hello to the world. */
import java.awt.Graphics;
import java.applet.Applet;

public class HelloApplet extends Applet {

    /* Make sure the applet is sized correctly. */
    public void init() {
        resize(200,60);
    }
    /* When the applet draws itself, greet the world. */
    public void paint(Graphics g) {
        g.drawString("Hello, world!", 60, 25);
    }


}
```

This code doesn't look too different from what we had before, does it? Maybe even a little simpler? One reason it's a little less complicated is that we don't have to create a top-level frame in which to display this application. We don't have to create an instance of anything at all—we don't even need a `main()` routine!

We can get away with this because the Web browser supplies a frame for us. It also instantiates our applet, so we don't have to do that ourselves inside `main()`. All we have to do is set up the user interface as we want it and respond to the events we're interested in. In this case, we override `init()` to size the window and respond to the `paint()` message by greeting the world.

Now, you may be asking yourself, "Just what window are we talking about? All I see is that we're creating an Applet subclass." Well, that's the beauty of applets. The Applet class inherits from class Panel, and, as you'll recall, you use panels to contain and arrange user interface components. So, an applet, in addition to being the framework of the application in a Web page, is also a user interface container in its own right.

Figure 8.1 shows what HelloApplet looks like when it runs in Windows 95.

Figure 8.1   HelloApplet running in Windows 95

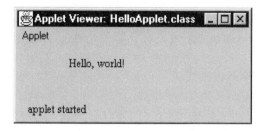

The Life Cycle of an Applet

What's happening with an applet compared with a stand-alone application is not as intuitive because your Applet instance is communicating closely with the Web browser. So what's the Web browser saying to your applet? And how does it need to respond?

When your applet is first loaded and run by the Web browser, the Web browser dispatches `init()` to the applet. This is the applet's chance to set up its user interface, initialize its data, size its window, and so on.

When your applet starts running, which is likely to be right away, the Web browser tells your applet to begin by calling its `start()` method. This is your applet's big chance to set up any objects it might need to perform its work. In particular, you might want to create any threads that your applet uses.

When the user leaves the Web page containing your applet, your applet will receive `stop()`. (The browser will also call this method if the user reloads your applet or quits the browser.) At this point, you can stop any threads that are running and perform any other processing that you might want to undertake to shut down your applet.

If the user reloads or restarts your applet, the browser will call `start()` again and your applet will live once more. If the user quits the browser, the browser will call your applet's `destroy()` method and you can perform any last minute cleanup.

Figure 8.2 shows how an applet lives its life, progressing through different states and responding to different milestones.

Figure 8.2   Applet life cycle

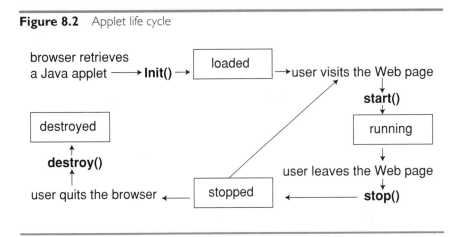

Preparing a Java Program for the Web

For simple programs (in particular, for those that do not create their own threads), it's fairly straightforward to get a Java application running over the Web. You don't need a main() routine anymore. Instead, you should respond to the appropriate method calls just listed as part of the applet life cycle. In particular, you may only need to override init(), as we did in the HelloApplet class.

Also, as pointed out, the Web browser itself provides the top-level frame for your application. All you need to do is arrange your user interface within your Applet instance, and you'll get hooked up to the Web browser's frame automatically.

If you wish, there's nothing stopping you from creating separate top-level frames to display other windows floating separately from the Web browser. Just create a frame as you did before, create and arrange its user interface, and use the show() method to make it appear.

Putting an Applet into a Web Page

Once you have a program that's all set to go on the Web, you'll need a Web page to contain it. To indicate to the browser that your HTML document contains a Java class, you use the tag <applet>, provide the keywords you'd like to include, and use </applet> at the end.

The keyword `code` specifies the class you'd like to execute. You can also use keywords to pass arguments to your applet. (Chapter 14 contains more information on applets and explains how this is done.)

Listing 8.2 gives an example of an HTML file that contains a Java applet.

Listing 8.2

```
<title>Hello, Applet!</title>
<hr>
<applet code=HelloApplet.class width=600 height=300>
</applet>
<hr>
<a href="HelloApplet.java">The source.</a>
```

Running an Applet

There are two basic ways to run your applet:

1. You can use the `appletviewer` command that comes with the Java Developers Kit (JDK). This allows you to run your application by providing a mini-browser environment. With this command, you can test your application without bringing up a full-blown browser application.
2. You can run your applet directly in a Java-enabled browser. Appendix A has all the platform-specific information and Web resources you'll need to get up and running on your environment.

■ A DESSERT TOPPING *AND* A FLOOR WAX

With only minor modifications, applets can run as stand-alone applications, which turns them into both applets *and* applications at the same time. The advantage of this approach is that you only need to maintain a single set of source files to have your classes run either stand-alone or over the Web.

Listing 8.3 shows the HelloApplet class modified to run in either environment. A discussion of the details follows this listing.

Listing 8.3

```
/* This applet can be run either within a Web browser
 * or as a stand-alone application.
 */
import java.awt.Graphics;
import java.awt.Frame;
import java.applet.Applet;

public class HelloEither extends Applet {

   public void init() {
      resize(200,60);
   }

   public void paint(Graphics g) {
      g.drawString("Hello, world!", 60, 25);
   }

   /** This main routine ensures this class will execute
     * whether it is run as an applet in a Web browser
     * or in a stand-alone environment.
     */
   public static void main(String args[]) {

      // This line only appears in the standard output
      // when this class is executed using the "java"
      // interpreter command.
      System.out.println("We are in main.");

      // Create an instance of this applet.
      HelloEither h = new HelloEither();
      h.init();

      // Create a frame in which to display this applet.
      Frame f = new Frame("Hello, World and Applet!");
      f.resize(200,60);

      // Add this applet to the frame and show the frame.
      f.add("Center", h);
      f.show();
   }

}
```

You can see that the top part of HelloEither is identical to HelloApplet, except that we've also imported class Frame. We need to do this because we have to create our own top-level container (a Frame instance) if we're going to run stand-alone—that is, if the Web browser isn't going to be around to supply a top-level frame for us. So, we create a Frame instance in the `main()` routine, which now gets executed because the interpreter needs to start somewhere.

In running stand-alone, we have to create our own Applet instance. We can add the Applet instance to the frame we create, show the frame, and voila! We have an applet running stand-alone.

The rest of this book uses this implementation approach for all the remaining applets.

■ WRITING SIMPLE OUTPUT

As before, displaying formatted output doesn't change the program too much. Check out Listing 8.4.

Listing 8.4

```
/* Display the Earth's escape velocity using a
 * graphical interface capable of running as
 * part of a Web page.
 */
import java.awt.Graphics;
import java.awt.Frame;
import java.applet.Applet;

public class EscapeApplet extends Applet {
   double velocity = 11.2;

   /** Set the applet to an initial screen size. */
   public void init() {
      resize(300,60);
   }

   /** When this applet redraws itself, display the
     * earth's escape velocity.
     */
   public void paint(Graphics g) {
      String string = "The Earth's escape velocity is " +
         velocity + " km/sec.";
      g.drawString(string, 30, 25);
   }
   /** Create a main routine so that this applet can
     * also be run using the Java interpreter.
     */
   public static void main(String args[]) {
      EscapeApplet esc = new EscapeApplet();
      esc.init();
```

```
        Frame f = new Frame("EscapeApplet");
        f.resize(300,60);

        f.add("Center", esc);
        f.show();
    }

}
```

▪ READING SIMPLE INPUT

Study Listing 8.5 to see how we've turned the PlanetaryScale application into an applet. The changes are along the lines of what we've already discussed. That is, we need to extend class Applet rather than class
Frame. Listing 8.5 also shows this class is ready to run as either an applet or a stand-alone application.

Listing 8.5

```
/* Displays an interface for calculating your weight on the moon.
 * This program is an applet that is intended to be run in a
 * Web browser that supports Java.
 * PlanetaryApplet - can be used as a basis for
 *      calculating your weight on a variety of planets
 *      throughout the solar system. In this version it
 *      calculates your weight on the moon.
 */
import java.awt.TextField;
import java.awt.Label;
import java.awt.Event;
import java.awt.Frame;
import java.applet.Applet;

public class PlanetaryApplet extends Applet {
    Label        label;
    TextField    textField;
    Astronaut    armstrong;
  /** Step onto the scale... */
    void calculateWeight() {
        armstrong = new Astronaut(getEarthWeight());
        showMoonWeight(armstrong.moonWeight());
    }

    /** Retrieve the value in the text field.
     * If the number was not typed in as an acceptable double, we
     * might get an exception. Be prepared to handle this so that
     * the program does not terminate.
     */
```

```
double getEarthWeight() {
  double wt;
  try {
    wt = Double.valueOf(textField.getText()).doubleValue();
  } catch (java.lang.NumberFormatException e) {
      wt = 0.0;
  }
  return wt;
}

/** Display the result to the user. */
void showMoonWeight(double f) {;
    label.setText("Your moon weight is " + String.valueOf(f));
}

/** Set up the user interface. This consists of a text field
  * for the user to enter a value, and a label to be used to
  * display a result.
  */
public void init() {
    resize(400,60);

    // Make the text field 6 columns wide.
    textField = new TextField(6);
    add(textField);

  label = new Label("Enter your earth weight into the field.");
  add(label);

    armstrong = new Astronaut(0.0);
}

/** Respond to user actions. When the user hits the return
  * key, Java dispatches an event. Return true if we handled
  * the event here, false otherwise so that someone else
  * up the window hierarchy can handle it.
  */
public boolean handleEvent(Event e) {
    if (e.target instanceof TextField && e.id ==
        Event.ACTUAL_EVENT) {
      calculateWeight();
      return true;
    }
    return false;
}

/** Be able to run stand-alone if necessary.
  * Instantiate the applet and set up a frame to
  * contain the applet.
  */
public static void main(String args[]) {
  PlanetaryApplet ps = new PlanetaryApplet();
  ps.init();
```

```
        // Create a top-level frame.
        Frame f = new Frame("PlanetaryApplet");
        f.resize(400,60);

        // Configure and display the window hierarchy.
        f.add("Center", ps);
        f.show();
    }

}
```

The PlanetaryScale applet (now called `PlanetaryApplet` to help avoid confusion) again, as before, uses the very same `Astronaut` class that we defined back in Chapter 6. Its code is repeated in Listing 8.6 for easy reference here.

Listing 8.6

```
/* Astronaut - a template for storing
 *        information on different astronauts.
 */
class Astronaut {
    Double earthWeight;

    /** Constructor */
    Astronaut (double weight) {
      earthWeight = new Double(weight);
    }

    /** The astronaut can calculate its weight on the moon. */
    public double moonWeight () {
      return earthWeight.doubleValue() * .166;
    }

}
```

■ GOING WITH THE FLOW

In the text-based PlanetaryScale application, the user was taken on a straight path from beginning to end (Figure 8.3).

When we created a window with user interface elements, this window remained on the screen until the user was through using it. When the user quit this window, the application ended. The path through the application became a little less direct (Figure 8.4).

Now that we have an applet, there's yet another wrinkle or two (Figure 8.5).

Figure 8.3 Flowchart for the text-based PlanetaryScale application

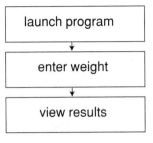

Figure 8.4 Flowchart for the graphical PlanetaryScale application

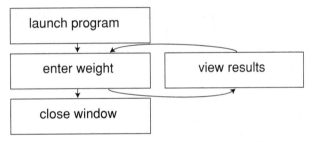

The Web browser never really destroys the applet until the user quits the Web browser. The browser loads and starts the applet, but if the user leaves the Web page that contains the applet, the applet is not unloaded. It just receives `stop()` and stops its processing. If the user returns to that

Figure 8.5 Flow chart for the Web-based PlanetaryScale application

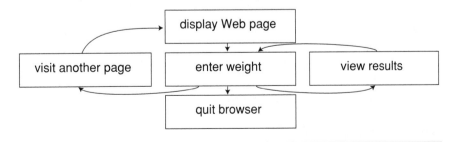

Web page, the same applet receives `start()`. That is, it receives `init()` and `destroy()` just once, but `start()` and `stop()` as many times as the user visits that Web page.

■ SUMMARY

This chapter showed you how to make your graphical Java applications run over the Web and, in doing so, rounded out the information given in Parts I and II.

Part I provided a conceptual grounding in Java from the perspective of C and C++. Part II gave you a quick start to programming Java by taking simple C and C++ programs and recreating them using Java. These programs included the canonical Hello, World application, an application that displayed formatted output, and a program that understood simple input.

■ WHAT'S NEXT?

Now that you've seen a bit of Java programming, you have an overall perspective that will help keep you on track as you delve into Java's details. Part III continues to relate Java programming to your knowledge of C and C++ and covers the implementation details for the concepts you've learned about so far.

PART III

Details

Part III contains many code snippets and explains a number of full-blown Java applications and applets. (See Chapter 1 for an overview of the applications described in this book and Appendix B for their complete listings.)

The chapters throughout Part III illustrate how to program in Java by presenting screenshots where appropriate, definitions of terms, and diagrams. As before, the approach taken here is to compare and contrast the languages to ground this new language (Java) in something familiar (C and C++).

Part III is organized as follows:

Chapter 9: Designing Your Classes: This chapter begins by looking at how to design the framework for your application: your class definitions and hierarchies, method declarations, and variable definitions.

Chapter 10: Implementing Your Classes: This chapter fills in the framework you developed in the previous chapter by examining how to implement methods.

Chapter 11: More Power to You: This chapter shows you how to implement unique features that are part of Java, such as synchronized multitasking and exceptions.

Chapter 12: Covering the Rest of It: The final chapter covering the language considers aspects of C++ that are *not* part of Java and teaches you what to do to instead.

Chapter 13: Working with Java's Packages: This chapter provides complete applications that illustrate how to use each of Java's primary packages.

Chapter 14: Writing for the Web: The closing chapter focuses on the Web and on special considerations when developing for the Web.

The chapters in Part III take an object-oriented approach, which is only natural since Java is an object-oriented language. By the end, you'll have crossed the bridge between C/C++ and Java and have explored some fun applications along the way.

9

Designing Your Classes

Chapter 9 provides the means for starting Java software development. It discusses the specifics of defining classes and their APIs. A number of the details of syntax and implementation will be quite familiar to C/C++ programmers; others will be new. By the time you've looked over this chapter, you'll know how to create the framework for your classes and your classes' data and behavior. In the next chapter, you'll fill in this framework with the methods necessary to let your classes and instances *do* something.

■ DEFINING CLASSES AND CREATING INSTANCES

Inheriting from Java's Classes

Your entire application is a collection of classes. You build all of your classes using Java's class framework. Java defines a base Object class from which all of its classes (and your own classes) are ultimately derived.

You can define a class that inherits from Java's Object class directly by using syntax like the following:

```
class ChocolateSundae extends Object {
    // ... your class information here
}
```

That is, where C++ uses the : notation to indicate the class you're subclassing, Java uses the `extends` keyword.

If you would rather inherit directly from a class other than class Object, then you specify that class's name instead of Object.

Java provides a great object framework, and you will be a part of it. Resistance is futile. Even if you try to not be a part of it, Java makes you a part of it. For example, if you define a class without telling Java which class you're extending, like this,

```
class MyClass {
}
```

then Java makes MyClass a subclass of class Object.

Classes are always accessible to any other class within the same package. (Packages are explained at the end of this chapter, but if you don't specifically define packages, all your classes are, by default, part of the same package.) If you have defined more than one package and you'd like your class to be accessible throughout your application, you can use the keyword `public`, as follows:

```
public class MyClass {
}
```

While you can have any number of public classes per package, you can have only one public class per source file. In addition, the source file that contains the public class must be named after that class. So, for example, the class MyClass would be contained in the source file `My-Class.java`.

Creating New Instances

In C++, you can define a new object along with the memory for the object simply by declaring it:

```
MyClass             myObject;
```

With this syntax, C++ will take care of freeing the allocated memory when the object goes out of scope. You can also use new to allocate memory for objects explicitly, obtaining a pointer to the object's location in memory:

```
MyClass     *myObject;
*myObject = new MyClass();
```

Using this approach, you must take care of freeing the object's memory yourself, like this:

```
delete myObject;
```

In some ways, Java uses a combination of these two options. In Java, you must declare the data type; you must use new to allocate the memory for the object; however, unlike C++, Java still takes care of freeing the memory when your program can no longer reference it:

```
MyClass myObject;
myObject = new MyClass();
```

Or, you can declare and allocate the object all in one line:

```
MyClass myObject = new MyClass();
```

All objects are allocated from a garbage-collected heap. While myObject in the Java example here refers to an object that exists in this garbage collected heap, you cannot treat myObject as a pointer or handle as you can in C++. You cannot cast this value to an integer or otherwise manipulate it in any way. In Java, all objects, including arrays and strings (which are discussed later in this book), are referred to by pointers that can't be corrupted because they cannot be manipulated as numbers.

■ CLASS AND INSTANCE DATA

Accessing Data

Just as in C++, you can access the data members in an object using the . operator:

```
int myInteger = myObject.instanceInteger;
```

You can do this for both instance and class data members.

As with C++, inside a method, you can refer to variables that belong to the current object without prefixing the variable with the object's reference. For example, if you have an object whose class definition looks like this,

```
class myClass {
    int number;
    void doubleTheNumber() {
        // ...
    }
}
```

then you can write code in `doubleTheNumber`() that looks like this:

```
number *= 2;
```

As you're used to in C++, this doubles the myClass object's lone instance variable. (We've jumped ahead here and looked at a small method. The Quick Start section already contained some examples of methods. By the end of this chapter and the next, you'll have become an expert on writing Java methods.)

What You Have to Work With

Java specifies a small set of data types that you can use to maintain your class and instance data. Each of your class and instance variables can be either a simple data type or a composite created out of Java's simple types:

1. *Simple data types* include: integer, floating-point, character, and boolean.
2. *Composite data types* include: classes, interfaces, and arrays.

(We'll talk about interfaces in this chapter and about arrays later.) There are no other kinds of composite types. There are no structures, unions, and so on. Just classes, interfaces, and arrays.

There are four different types of ***integers:***

1. `byte` is for signed 8-bit numbers.
2. `short` is for signed 16-bit numbers.

3. int is for signed 32-bit numbers.

4. long is for signed 64-bit numbers.

There is no unsigned keyword as there is in C/C++; all numbers are signed.

There are two types of *floating-point* numbers:

1. float is for signed 32-bit numbers.

2. double is for signed 64-bit numbers.

Characters (type char) are Unicode characters, which means they are 2 bytes long, not 1, as they are with ASCII characters in C and C++.

Boolean values (type boolean) indicate true or false. (Unlike C/C++, the values of true and false are part of the Java language.)

These values are guaranteed to use a particular amount of storage. int values, for example, will be 4 bytes; long values will be 8 bytes. This is quite different from C and C++, which do not specify as part of the language how much memory they will hold and can be different from one platform to the next.

All simple data types are *statically* typed. That is, all data types must be known at compile time. Objects, which are composites of simple types and other composites, are *dynamically* typed. That is, they can be determined at runtime so that your code can do different things with different types of objects.

Some Basics

The equivalent of C++ class and instance data members are Java class and instance variables. *Class variables* are automatically initialized when you load a class. *Instance variables* are initialized when you instantiate a class. If you don't define default values for your variables, your variables will be set to 0 for numbers, null for objects, and false for Booleans.

In Java, variable names must start with a letter, a dollar sign ($), or an underscore (_). Other than this, they can consist of almost any Unicode character.

Wrappers

Sometimes you'll want to work with a particular number as a full-blown object so that you can, for example, ask it to "return your representation as a string" or ask "What is your integer equivalent?" To do this, Java defines a variety of *wrapper* objects that turn working with simple data types (such as numbers) into dealing with actual, intelligent objects. Java's wrapper types include the basic data types: Integer, Long, Float, Double, Character, and Boolean.

You can create a wrapper instance by providing the data it represents:

```
Integer myInteger = new Integer(123);
Character myCharacter = new Character('z');
```

Type wrappers provide all sorts of useful methods. Primarily, these include obtaining the data as different types and converting to and from character strings. For example, you can ask an Integer instance for its values as a double:

```
double d = myInteger.doubleValue();
```

And you can convert a value to a string like this:

```
String s = myInteger.toString();
```

One useful technique you can implement with wrappers is to set up a chain of method invocations to convert data input using the keyboard to numeric types. For example, if you have a StringBuffer containing the characters the user entered, you can convert this to a double data type as follows:

1. Create a String instance to represent the value in the String-Buffer.
2. Use a Double's `valueOf()` class method to create a new Double instance.
3. Use the wrapper's `doubleValue()` instance method to return the double value this new Double instance maintains.

Putting it all together, you get

```
double d = Double.valueOf(buffer.toString()).doubleValue();
```

One thing to be aware of with this technique is that Java might throw an exception if the StringBuffer does not convert into a double. You should be prepared to handle this situation.

Instance Variables

Here's an example of defining data that is maintained by each instance of a class:

```
class AfricanElephant {
   float tuskLength;
}
```

By default, an instance of any subclass of AfricanElephant, in addition to an instance of AfricanElephant itself, can get access to this variable.

If you want different access control, there are a number of keywords you can use to specify which objects are allowed to access this variable.

public—Any class, regardless of which package it is in, can access an instance variable defined as public.

private—Only an instance of the class defining the variable can ever access it. Not even instances of its subclasses can get to it.

protected—Only instances of the class defining the variable and instances of its subclasses can access the variable.

(blank)—This is accessible from anywhere within the same package. (It is the default.)

Class Variables

To associate a variable with a class rather than with each instance of a class, you can, as in C++, declare the variable to be static.

```
class AfricanElephant {
   static int population;
   float tuskLength;
}
```

As with instance variables, you can use all the same keywords to specify access to your instance data.

Constants

If you have defined an instance variable that you don't want overridden, ever, you can specify that this variable is `final`. It's like putting a lock on it. One great way to use final variables is as constants, especially when coupled with public class variables in public classes so that they are available throughout your application. For example, you can write

```
public static final NUM_STATES = 50;
```

That way, when Puerto Rico becomes a state, you can easily update to 51 without looking all over your code for where you hard-coded 50. Further, if you defined this constant (there are no constants, per se, in Java, but let's call a duck a duck) in a public class called America, you can then access this constant from anywhere, like this:

```
America.NUM_STATES
```

You'll notice that Java defines a number of constants. For example, there's a constant called PI in its Math class that you can reference by writing

```
Math.PI
```

There are also constant objects that you can reference. For example, there are color objects that you can get via the Color class, like this:

```
Color.red
Color.blue
Color.yellow
```

Because these variables are declared as `final`, you cannot replace the color red with a nice taupe, even though you might be an interior decorator. And you don't have to worry about a particular platform's definition of red because the use of class libraries frees you from this detail.

Static Initializers

Another cool thing about class variables is that you can set up *initializer code* to initialize your class variables when your class is first loaded. An example is provided in Listing 9.1.

Listing 9.1

```
class Cloud {
    public static void main(String args[]) {
        System.out.println("main");
        Cirrus c = new Cirrus();
    }
}

class Cirrus {
    static int arr[] = new int[3];
    static {
        System.out.println("static initializer");
        for (int i = 0; i < arr.length; i++)
            arr[i] = i;
        }

    Cirrus() {
        System.out.println("constructor");
        for (int i = 0; i < arr.length; i++)
            System.out.println(arr[i]);
    }
}
```

The output for this program that appears on the standard output device (that is, your screen) is

```
main
static initializer
constructor
0
1
2
```

As you can see, as soon as the class Cirrus is referenced, it's loaded into memory. At that time, before an instance is created, its static initializer code is executed to set its class variables.

Since classes are loaded dynamically (as needed by the interpreter), you can make forward-references to methods and classes that aren't yet known to the runtime system. For example, your static initializer can refer to other unloaded classes. If you do this, then your class will stop initializing until Java loads the class to which you refer. If you get a little too creative and refer back to a class that's waiting for another class to load, Java throws an exception (in particular, `NoClassDefFoundException`).

Another kind of illegal forward-dependency is something like this:

```
int i = 2 + j;
int j = 3;
```

This code shows two instance variables, but the first one refers to the second, which hasn't been defined yet. However, since static variables are initialized when a class is loaded, the following code is perfectly legal (if a little confusing):

```
int i = 2 + j;
static int j = 3;
```

■ CLASS AND INSTANCE METHODS

So that's how you set up your classes to maintain data. What about defining behavior?

Java takes a different approach from C++ regarding the default inheritance for a method. C++ defaults to nonvirtual. This is the right decision for efficiency's sake. Java chooses to default to virtual (though there's no keyword to indicate this)—that is, inherited by subclasses and able to be overridden. This is the right decision in terms of "what you'd expect." That is, in an object-oriented language, you'd expect your subclasses to inherit the behavior of their ancestors. In Java, you have to make an extra effort to optimize if you don't want this behavior.

This section explains how to define the interfaces to your methods. In the next chapter, you'll learn more of how to write the actual code that gives your methods behavior.

Calling Methods

First of all, calling a method looks just as it does in C++. You append the method name onto the instance or class that will respond and put the parameters in parentheses. Of course, methods can return results:

```
result = myInstance.myMethod(parameterA, parameterB);
```

If the method you're calling returns an object that you use purely as an intermediary result, you can append another call right onto the first one:

```
secondResult = myInstance.myFirstMethod().mySecondMethod();
```

In this example, `myInstance` defines a method called `myFirst-Method()` that returns an object. This object defines a method called `mySecondMethod()`, which returns a result that we can assign to a data type we've called `secondResult`. (You don't have to worry about any memory leaks here because Java will garbage-collect the object returned by `myFirstMethod()` when it sees you can no longer reference the object from your application.)

Instance Methods

To give your classes new behavior, you define new methods. (You can also change the behavior of inherited methods, which we'll describe shortly.) To define a new method, you write it just as you would a C++ inline method, as follows:

```
class MyClass {
   void newMethod() {
      // ... your code here
   }
}
```

Note that "inline" here means an inline *method*, not a C/C++ inline *function* declared with the `inline` keyword. There is no way to create an inline function directly in Java. However, there is a way to hint to the Java compiler that you want your method code to appear in place throughout your application. (Check out Chapter 12 for information on this kind of optimization.)

Usually, in C++, you define the interface to your object and then separately define your method code. You might do something like this:

```
class MyClass {
   void newMethod();
};

MyClass::newMethod()
{
}
```

If you wanted to put newMethod() inline, you'd declare MyClass by writing something like this:

```
class MyClass {
protected:
   void newMethod() { /* your code here */ }
};
```

In C++, the guideline is to do this only if the method is small. In Java, all methods are written this way. In other words, you do not define your method's interface in one location and its implementation somewhere else; in Java, both are defined together.

You should always declare a return value, unless you are creating a constructor method. In the example just given, we have no return value, so we indicate this by using void.

The keywords you can place on methods to control who can execute it are identical to the keywords available for variables.

Class Methods

To associate behavior with a class rather than with an instance of a class, you can define the method to be static:

```
static void newMethod() {
}
```

As with instance methods, you can use all the same keywords to specify which other classes and instances can execute your class method.

Method Parameters

Simple data types are passed by value. Objects, however, are passed by reference. That is, if you pass an object into a method, you can change the object's variables. The calling method will see all the object's changed fields when the method returns.

The example given in Listing 9.2 shows some details of passing an object to a method. While you can change the values inside an object, you can't change the object itself. (To keep track of the object, we're displaying its hash code. Java assigns each object a unique identifier at runtime. This number is stored as the object's hash code.)

Listing 9.2

```java
public class MyClass1 {
   static public void main(String args[]) {
      MyClass1 mc1 = new MyClass1();
      MyDataClass mdc = new MyDataClass();

      System.out.println("main: hash code = " + mdc.hashCode());
      mdc.myData = 1;
      System.out.println("main: mdc.myData = " + mdc.myData);
      mc1.test1(mdc);
      System.out.println("main: mdc.myData = " + mdc.myData);
      mc1.test2(mdc);
      System.out.println("main: hash code = " + mdc.hashCode());
      System.out.println("main: mdc.myData = " + mdc.myData);
   }

   void test1(MyDataClass mdc) {
      System.out.println("test1: hash code = " + mdc.hashCode());
      mdc.myData = 2;
   }
   void test2(MyDataClass mdc) {
      System.out.println("test2: hash code = " + mdc.hashCode());
      mdc = new MyDataClass();
      System.out.println("test2: hash code = " + mdc.hashCode());
      mdc.myData = 3;
   }
}

class MyDataClass {
   public int myData;
}
```

When you execute MyClass1, the output is

```
main: hash code = -292489336
main: mdc.myData = 1
test1: hash code = -292489336
main: mdc.myData = 2
test2: hash code = -292489336
test2: hash code = -292488872
main: hash code = -292489336
main: mdc.myData = 2
```

As you can see, when the object is passed into `test1()` and we change a variable in this object, the change appears in the caller as well. (However, when we try to replace the object passed to `test2()` with a new object, that change does not travel outside the called method. The new object created in `test2()` would eventually be garbage-collected.) Note that your hash-code values are likely to be different than mine since they are determined at runtime.

Overloading Methods

As with C++, you can overload methods in Java. As you're already aware, while method names can overlap, method signatures (the number of parameters and their types) must be unique.

For example, you can define two methods with the same name but a different number of parameters:

```
// method with 1 parameter
void explode(int duration) { }

// method with 2 parameters
void explode(int duration, int intensity) { }
```

You can also define a method with the same number of parameters as a method you already defined (just make certain the parameter types are different):

```
// another method with 1 parameter
void explode(boolean playSound) { }
```

You can also overload constructor names. The beginning of the next chapter contains some examples of this.

■ INHERITANCE

Class Hierarchies

It's through inheritance that object-oriented languages encourage code reuse. As your application grows, you can extend the classes you've already created to add new behavior. To help with this, you can push common behavior up the class hierarchy to where it can be shared by the greatest number of classes.

You always use Java's classes as your base classes. You can hook into Java's class hierarchy in a number of places. To help you get oriented, here are the four classes you'll extend most often:

1. Extend *Object* when you only want the basic behavior for a class.
2. Extend *Applet* when you create your own applet to run via a Web browser.
3. Extend *Thread* to implement another thread of control.
4. Extend *Panel* to organize your user interface.

One more note about hierarchies: You can indicate that "the buck stops here" and a hierarchy comes to an end by using the keyword `final` in a class definition. Using `final` makes the class impossible to subclass.

Abstract and Concrete Classes

Abstract classes can help you design class hierarchies. Abstract classes are usually defined when you want to group related classes together by having them descend from the same superclass, but at least one method in this common superclass depends on the specifics of the subclasses themselves.

For example, you might want to create a virtual zoo. You know you want Tigers and Penguins and Kangaroos. You know all these animals share at least some behavior, but this behavior might be particular to the animal involved. For example, all these animals can move, but a tiger prowls, a penguin waddles, and a kangaroo hops. These animals also share particular attributes, such as the top speed at which they move.

You can declare a class called `Animal` that contains the variable to maintain the animal's top speed, and you can declare a placeholder for a method that will describe how they move.

Since you will never instantiate Animal directly, Animal is an abstract class. Any class that declares an abstract method, or that inherits from an abstract class and does not make that method concrete, is an abstract class:

```
abstract class Animal {
    public int topSeed;
    abstract void move();
}
```

Declaring a class as `abstract` makes instantiating that class illegal. For the Animal class, subclasses must ultimately supply behavior for the `move()` method. At the point that `move()` is implemented, that subclass and all subsequent subclasses can then be instantiated (unless one of these subclasses again defines an abstract method):

```
class Kangaroo extends Animal {
    void move() {
    }
}
// ...

Animal kanga = new Kangaroo();
kanga.move();
```

There are also some rules for the keywords you are allowed to place on an abstract method. You have to use the keywords in ways that make sense. For example, you can't make a private method abstract (since you can never override it!); you can't override an abstract method with another abstract method (since this wouldn't do anything!); at some point in your application, you must have a subclass that implements the abstract method if you wish to instantiate the class and call its method; also, static methods and constructors can't be abstract.

Interfaces

You can only implement single inheritance in Java. However, Java provides a mechanism for achieving some of the benefits of multiple inheritance without the inherent problems of traversing a complex class hierarchy that results from multiple inheritance. Java's substitute is to allow your classes to share characteristics through the use of a type of abstract class called an *interface*.

Interfaces are best used for defining "has a" types of relationships. That is, interfaces allow you to sprinkle characteristics into your class hierarchy. Classes are better used for defining "is a" relationships.

For example, you might have a StreetAddress class that keeps track of a street and a house number. You might also have a City class that maintains a city in the United States. What would you do about a Location class? Does it inherit from both StreetAddress and City since it shares similar properties?

A better alternative is to decide that Location is not an *example* of a StreetAddress and a City at all; rather, a Location has the *properties* of a StreetAddress and City. One possible design might be to create interfaces out of StreetAddress and City and allow Location to implement their specific data and behaviors.

For another example, suppose you want to provide some behavior for your zoo animals that depends on whether the animal has eight legs. Octopi and scorpions probably will not share the same ancestors, but they both might share characteristics of an octopod.

One way to define these characteristics is to create a completely abstract class—that is, an interface. Interfaces automatically set any data they define to `public` and `final` and so must be assigned a value in the interface definition. Interfaces only provide the APIs for methods; classes that implement an interface must supply an implementation for the APIs they inherit. Here's an example from the subatomic world:

```
interface ElectricallyCharged {
   int units = 3;     // electric charge is charge()/units
   int charge();
}

class TopQuark implements ElectricallyCharged {
   static public void main(String args[]) {
   }
   public int charge() {
      return 2;
   }
}
```

Note that `charge()` must be declared as `public`.

As with classes, interfaces can be declared without any keywords, in which case they're available to any other class in the same package. If you declare an interface as `public`, it's available to any class in your application.

You can create hierarchies of interfaces by defining other interfaces that inherit from base interfaces by extending them:

```
interface ElectricallyCharged {
}

interface Quark extends ElectricallyCharged {
}
```

Interfaces are (more or less) exceptions to the rule that everything must inherit, eventually, from Java's class hierarchy. Interfaces do not fit into Java's class hierarchy by default, though you can extend one of Java's predefined interfaces if you wish.

If you do not fully implement an interface, you must declare your class as `abstract`, and some other subclass of your abstract class must implement any unimplemented methods. The example in Listing 9.3 shows this in action, as well as the fact that you can ask a particular instance if it inherits from an interface. This can be particularly useful before calling a method to which it might not be able to respond.

Listing 9.3

```
class Collider {
    public static void main(String args[]) {
        TopQuark q = new TopQuark();

        System.out.println("ElectricallyCharged? " + (q instanceof
ElectricallyCharged));
        System.out.println("Quark? " + (q instanceof Quark));
        System.out.println("TopQuark? " + (q instanceof TopQuark));

        if (q instanceof ElectricallyCharged)
            System.out.println("q.units = " + q.units);
    }
}

interface ElectricallyCharged {
    int units = 3;
    int charge();
}
```

```
abstract class Quark implements ElectricallyCharged {
}

class TopQuark extends Quark {
   public int charge() {
      return 2;
   }
}
```

Here's the output:

```
ElectricallyCharged? true
Quark? true
TopQuark? true
e.units = 3
```

If you would like a class to implement more than one interface, you can simply list these interfaces one after the other, as in the following code:

```
class Star implements Fusion, Mass, Rotation {
}

interface Fusion {
}

interface Mass {
}

interface Rotation {
}
```

Inheriting Variables

As with C++, you can refer to inherited variables simply by using their names. Inherited variables include those declared as protected or public. There's no way you can get at a private variable from a class other than the one that defines it. Subclasses can't even get to it by casting or using super. Only methods that run in the context of the class that defines the private variable can access it.

The scoping rules in the next chapter provide information on accessing variables with the same name in your own ancestor and distinguishing between local variables and instance variables with the same name.

Overriding Existing Methods

Subclasses can override any `public` or `protected` method in one of their ancestor methods. (Subclasses can also override a method if it's left set to the default access privilege, which allows any class in the same package to access it.)

To override a method, all you need to do is write the method over again for your new class, declaring it and defining code for it just as you would for a brand new method. Define your method in place. Make sure you match the parameters of the method you're overriding, or Java will think you're defining a new method. And don't forget to match the return value as well.

To execute the inherited behavior, you must pass the call up the class hierarchy. To do this, you can use the `super` variable. This variable is valid in any instance method and indicates the object that's the direct ancestor of the current object. That is, `super` represents the superclass of `this`. Here's a quick example:

```
class Tree {
    int grow() {
        // ... your grow method here ...
    }
}

class Pine extends Tree {
    int grow() {
        super.grow();
        // ... your grow method here ...
    }
}
```

When you override a method, you cannot make it more private than it already is. That is, you can't take a `public` method and reimplement it as `protected` or `private`.

The only way you can change access to a method is by turning an inherited, `protected` method into a `public` method. But still, you can only call the inherited method from a subclass. Listing 9.4 gives an example of changing a `protected` method to a `public` method.

Listing 9.4

```
class Tree {
    protected void growsInBrooklyn() {
        System.out.println("A tree grows in Brooklyn");
```

```
    }
    public static void main(String args[]) {
        Birch b = new Birch();
        b.growsInBrooklyn();
    }
}

class Birch extends Tree {
    public void growsInBrooklyn() {
        System.out.println("A birch grows in Brooklyn");
        super.growsInBrooklyn();
    }
}
```

The output for this forest is

```
A birch grows in Brooklyn
A tree grows in Brooklyn
```

The only time you do not need to explicitly call the inherited behavior—even when you want it executed—is when you create a constructor. (You can call your ancestor's constructor if you want to, however. See the beginning of the next chapter for more information concerning how to implement constructors.)

Note that even if a subclass did not redefine an inherited method, as in

```
class MySuperclass {
    void myMethod() {
    }
}

class MySubclass extends MySuperclass {
}
```

you could still call myMethod() on an instance of MySubclass. In that case, myMethod() would get passed up the ancestor chain automatically until someone handled it.

Subclasses cannot override private or final methods. However, there is a slight difference between what happens if a subclass *tries* to override one of these. For example, if you define

```
class MySuperclass {
    final void myFinal() {
    }
}
```

you cannot create a subclass of MySuperclass and define another method called `myFinal()`. The compiler will complain if you attempt to do so, which is pretty much what you would expect.

While `private` methods are similar in the sense that you cannot override them, there is a twist. If you define

```
class MySuperclass {
   private void myPrivate() {
   }
}
```

you can still define a subclass like this:

```
class MySubclass extends MySuperclass {
   private void myPrivate() {
   }
}
```

The version of `myPrivate()` that will execute depends on the class type that handles the method. There's no way to pass `myPrivate()` up from MySubclass to MySuperclass: Neither casting to MySuperclass nor using `super` will work. The compiler will complain that MySuperclass does not define such a method. Of course, it does; however, it's not available outside the class.

Casting Classes

You can cast between classes if you need to. Casting to a class that's your ancestor is called *narrowing*. Casting to a subclass is called *widening*. You cannot cast to sibling classes that are not part of the same branch of the class hierarchy for the object that you're casting.

You might want to cast if a particular calling sequence expects an object of a certain type. For example, you can write

```
class TasteTester {
   void sip(Object input) {
      if (input instanceof FrenchRoast)
         drink((FrenchRoast)input);
      if (input instanceof StaleBeans)
         throwAway((StaleBeans)input);
   }
}
```

This class either drinks some coffee or throws it away if it's stale. If the methods for `drink()` and `throwAway()` expect instances of FrenchRoast and StaleBeans, respectively, we can make them happy by casting.

■ ORGANIZING YOUR CLASSES

Compiling creates a different `.class` file for each class, even if the source for all of your classes is kept in the same `.java` file. For example, if you implemented class Bird, class Wren, and class CactusWren all in the same source file, Java would still create a separate class file for each of them. Java has to do this because, remember, you execute classes, not files. If Java had to load additional classes into the runtime environment, Java would be able to do this efficiently since each class's byte codes are stored in its own file.

Even though you have separate files for each compiled class, you can bring some order to your collection of class files by creating packages.

Creating Packages

By default, all classes are accessible only within the package in which they're defined. If you don't explicitly define a package for your classes, then they belong to a package called `Default`. Another way to look at it is that, by default, any class in your application can access any other class.

This implies that your classes are, in fact, available only within the *application* in which they're defined. If you would like to share your classes across multiple applications, you can create groups of classes called packages. You can then import your *package* into the application where you want to use it.

To create a package, define the package name at the top of your Java source file:

```
package SubAtomicParticles;
```

The Java compiler will place all of the classes defined in this source file into this (new or existing) package.

Accessing Classes

If you would like to access a class outside the package in which it's defined, you must declare that class to be `public`:

```
public class YourClass extends ImmediateSuperclass {
}
```

While you can have as many classes defined in a Java source file as you'd like to, you can have only one `public` class per file. For this reason, it can sometimes be easier to maintain your project if you define only one class per file.

When you want to use classes in another package, you import either the one class you're interested in or the entire package. To import one particular class, specify this class after the package name:

```
import SubAtomicParticles.Proton;
```

To import all the classes in a package, use the wild-card notation:

```
import SubAtomicParticles.*;
```

You can use the classes in SubAtomicParticles in as many applications as you'd like to. For example, you can import these particles into a nuclear reactor application as well as a supercollider simulator. Now code reuse is *really* working for you!

■ PROTOTYPING (PART 1)

The first section of this book mentioned that the design philosophy of a language should, ideally, encourage you to write good code. Even when you dive right in and start hacking, the Java language helps you put stakes in the ground, as it were, to mark the guideposts and perimeter of your application. So, let's start applying some of the things we learned to build an application by taking advantage of Java's object-oriented approach.

Consider an application that will perform some calculations related to Einstein's special theory of relativity. Hah! You forgot to take that course? No problem! We'll create a class called `Einstein` that will know just what to do.

Here's the project: Allow the user to enter a spaceship speed that is a certain percentage of the speed of light. Einstein will calculate how long it will take to reach a particular galaxy—in this case, Andromeda, which is approximately 2.2-million light-years away.

First, we want to be able to ask Einstein a question. So, we'll need to be able to execute the Einstein class. Recall that, to execute a class from the command line, we need to define the `main()` class method:

```
class Einstein {
    static public void main(String[] args) {
    }
}
```

Keep in mind that this little snippet will compile just fine, though at the moment it won't do much. The point is that almost every new line of code we write will still allow our application to compile (as long as all our brackets line up). That is, as we define new classes and methods, we add to the application's architecture without breaking the program. This is fantastic for prototyping.

We'll want Einstein to explain what it's doing and show some results. To this end, we can define a placeholder method for showing instructions and results:

```
static void showInstructions() {
}

static void showResults() {
}
```

Since we're calculating a time value to show—in particular, the time to travel from here to Andromeda as we experience it en route—we'll probably want to pass this time value to the `showResults()` method. So, `showResults()` should look like this instead:

```
static void showResults(double time) {
}
```

We're defining these methods as `static` so that we do not need to create an instance of Einstein to run the application.

One of the things we're going to do is get some input from the user. We'll ask the user to provide the speed the spaceship is traveling as a percentage of the speed of light (to make input as simple as possible). Let's write the framework for this.

When you read from the standard input, either you have to be prepared to handle I/O errors yourself, or you have to indicate that you won't handle them at all. If you don't want to handle them, indicate that the method might throw an I/O exception:

```
static double getPercentC()
     throws java.io.IOException {
}
```

At this point, we've defined the primary actions required by our application: provide instructions, get the necessary input, show the results. Now, we must decide where we will perform the calculations and which object will maintain the data we need.

Before you shout that Einstein is a pretty smart class and so should know how to do everything, keep in mind that one of the philosophies behind an object-oriented design is to "spread the intelligence around." Let's take this philosophy to heart and think about the elements in this application.

When we perform the calculation, Einstein is thinking about a few things, which are real parts of the model we're creating. These include a spaceship to do the traveling, the speed of light, and the far-off galaxy to which we're traveling. So, let's try creating instances to represent these things. In particular, let's create a SpaceShip class, a Light class, and a Galaxy class. One of the nice things about Java is that it's easy to give this idea a spin.

For starters, the Light class can maintain the knowledge that the speed of light is 2.998 times 10^8 meters per second (the C in Cm_s is meant to remind us that we're dealing with the speed of light, which is usually represented mathematically by C; the m_s part is for "meters per second"):

```
class Light {
   public static final double Cm_s = 2.998E8;
}
```

The SpaceShip class can maintain a speed and know how to determine the time dilation that occurs when it's traveling a certain number of light-years:

```
class SpaceShip {
   double speed;

   double calcTimeDilation(double distanceLightYr) {
   }
}
```

Let's run with this. Since the speed of light is the maximum velocity allowed by Einstein's formulas, we might want to throw an exception if the user enters a velocity faster than light. One way to indicate this condition is to define our own exception and specify that the method throws this exception if it is asked to perform a calculation it can't handle:

```
double calcTimeDilation(double distanceLightYr)
   throws WarpException {
}
```

We also need to define this exception class:

```
class WarpException extends Exception {
}
```

(Note that there's plenty more concerning exceptions in Chapter 11.)

One more thing for our initial framework: So that we don't hard-code a destination, let's define a Galaxy class that we can ask for information, such as how far away it is:

```
abstract class Galaxy {
   abstract public double getDistance();
}
```

Subclasses will implement `getDistance()` to return the distance in light-years from the earth.

So what do we have? Let's throw in some comments and look at the outline for this application so far (Listing 9.5).

Listing 9.5

```java
/** The Einstein class is pretty smart. You tell it what fraction
  * of the speed of light you're traveling to the Andromeda
  * galaxy, and Einstein tells you how long the trip will appear
  * to you, taking relativistic effects (i.e., time dilation) into
  * account.
  */
class Einstein {
   static public void main(String[] args) {
   }

   /** Tell the user how this program works.
     */
   static void showInstructions() {
   }

   /** Get input from the user.
     */
   static double getPercentC()
        throws java.io.IOException {
   }

   /** Tell the user the results of the calculation.
     */
   static void showResults(double time) {
   }
}

/** Light maintains the value of C.
  */
class Light {
   public static final double Cm_s = 2.998E8;      // meters/second
}

/** SpaceShip instances maintain a speed and know about
  * time dilation.
  */
class SpaceShip {
   double speed;      // the speed this ship is traveling

   /** Constructor to create a spaceship traveling at a
     * speed relative to the speed of light.
     */
   SpaceShip(double percent) {
   }

   /** Determine the time required to travel a distance in the
     * moving time frame, given the speed maintained by this ship.
     */
   double calcTimeDilation(double distanceLightYr)
      throws WarpException {
   }
```

```
    }

    /** An abstract class to define the API for galaxies.
      */
    abstract class Galaxy {
       abstract public double getDistance();
    }

    /** Thrown if the user has requested warp speed.
      */
    class WarpException extends Exception {
    }
```

■ SUMMARY

In this chapter, you worked through how to use Java to define an application's framework. That is, you now know how to define your classes and your classes' and instances' data and behavior. We even defined the framework for an application based on the principles of the most brilliant person who lived this century. Pretty good for a simple language. Let's move on to how the guts of classes are written and see how fast we need to travel to reach Andromeda in our lifetime.

■ WHAT'S NEXT?

Now that you have the skeleton arranged for your application, the next chapter shows you how to fill it in. While the Quick Start chapters took you to the moon, by the end of Chapter 10, you'll be zipping out of our galaxy and into the next!

10

Implementing Your Classes

Now that you know what your classes will do, it's time to start implementing the code. Chapter 10 continues to fill out the Java language by providing examples of how to construct instances, work with Java's data types, use operators, and control the flow through a Java program.

■ CREATING INSTANCES

Constructors

Just as in C++, you can write constructors if you want to execute your own code when new instances are created. Constructors take on the class name and never return a value.

If you don't create your own constructor, one will automatically be created for you that calls your immediate ancestor's constructor. This default constructor does not take any parameters, and, if you could see it, it would look something like this:

```
YourClass() {
   super();
}
```

This allows you to create new instances of your classes, as we've been doing so far in this book:

```
YourClass yc = new YourClass();
```

That's the only constructor you'll get by default, however. If you want to use a parameter or a set of parameters to initialize your object, you must overload (or override as appropriate) the constructor.

As a practical example, let's say you have a subclass of a Java class called a `Frame`. A Frame displays a window on the screen and contains other user interface elements. Optionally, this window can contain a title. If you want to create an instance of a Frame subclass called My-Frame and pass it a String so that it will display a title in the window, you have to create your own constructor. This new constructor you create will take one String parameter. All the constructor needs to do is call the constructor it inherits from Frame that accepts a String. You can write your new constructor like this:

```
MyFrame(String s) {
    super(s);
}
```

If you want to be fancy, you can also call another one of your own constructors. Suppose you have a constructor that takes a parameter to initialize a variable. But perhaps there's a lot of code in another constructor that you'd also like to execute. You can do it like this:

```
MyClass() {
    // common code
}

MyClass(int a) {
    // do something with a
    this();
}
```

Notice in this example that the constructor `MyClass()` does not call its superclass's constructor. You can either call the ancestor's constructor yourself or let the system do it for you. If you include `super()` in your constructor, the system won't call your ancestor's constructor again.

For example, consider Listing 10.1.

Listing 10.1

```
class FlyingMachine {
   FlyingMachine() {
      System.out.println("constructor for FlyingMachine");
   }
}

class Helicopter extends FlyingMachine {
   Helicopter() {
      System.out.println("constructor for Helicopter");
   }

   static public void main(String args[]) {
      new Helicopter();
   }
}
```

This program prints out

```
constructor for FlyingMachine
constructor for Helicopter
```

and is equivalent to

```
class FlyingMachine {
   FlyingMachine() {
      System.out.println("constructor for FlyingMachine");
   }
}

class Helicopter extends FlyingMachine {
   Helicopter() {
      super();
      System.out.println("constructor for Helicopter");
   }
   static public void main(String args[]) {
      new Helicopter();
   }
}
```

You also have to call the ancestor first thing if you create your own constructor, which stops you from calling it twice. (The second time you try to call it, it wouldn't be the first line of code in your constructor anymore, would it?)

By the way, remember that your instance and class variables are initialized for you to 0, null, and false, as appropriate. So, there's no need to create your own constructor simply to set your variables to these default values.

= and clone()

In C++, one nifty thing you can do is to override the = operator for a class. For example, you can define `operator=` so that it makes a copy of your object. You usually do this to manage memory allocations, including strings, that take place inside an object. This managing of memory is necessary mostly to ensure that when the object is freed the appropriate memory is freed, as well.

In Java, this is not an issue. Java manages the memory, so you won't get into trouble with double allocations or freeing memory that has already been freed. What's more, the only operator that's overloaded, you'll recall, is the + operator so that this operator works for math operations and for strings.

In Java, if you assign one object to another object, you have two choices: You can use either the = operator or the `clone()` method.

Listing 10.2 shows an example of using the = operator.

Listing 10.2

```
class MyClass {
    public static void main(String args[]) {
        City c1 = new City("Albany");
        State s1 = new State("New York", c1);
        s1.print();
        City c2 = new City("Austin");
        State s2 = new State("Texas", c2);
        s2.print();
        s2 = s1;
        s2.print();
    }
}

class State {
    String name;
    City capital;
    State(String s, City c) {
        name = s;
        capital = c;
    }
    void print() {
        System.out.println("State = " + name);
        System.out.println("Capital = " + capital.name);
        System.out.println("State hashcode = " + hashCode());
```

```
        System.out.println("Capital hashcode = " +
            capital.hashCode());
        System.out.println("");
    }
}

class City {
    String name;
    City(String s) {
        name = s;
    }
}
```

As you'd expect, when we print out `s2` after the assignment, it now refers to the object `s1`. The output is

```
State = New York
Capital = Albany
State hashcode = 21640144
Capital hashcode = 21640096

State = Texas
Capital = Austin
State hashcode = 21640488
Capital hashcode = 21640464

State = New York
Capital = Albany
State hashcode = 21640144
Capital hashcode = 21640096
```

You use `clone()` to have the system allocate a new object from memory and perform a bitwise copy of all the values and objects in the instance variables of the copied object into the new object. Since `clone()` specifically returns a data type that's an Object, you need to cast it to the class type you're using. For example, changing the line in MyClass's `main()` method from

```
s2 = s1;
```

to

```
s2 = (State)s1.clone();
```

yields the following output:

```
State = New York
Capital = Albany
```

```
State hashcode = 21640144
Capital hashcode = 21640096

State = Texas
Capital = Austin
State hashcode = 21640488
Capital hashcode = 21640464

State = New York
Capital = Albany
State hashcode = 21640688
Capital hashcode = 21640096
```

As you can see, `clone()` creates and allocates a brand new State instance. However, in performing the bitwise copy, the City object that stores the capital comes across unaffected and is identical to the original.

■ WORKING WITH DATA TYPES

Variable declarations can occur anywhere. You've already learned about some of the simple and composite data types. Here are some more details.

Integer

As in C++, the three ways to represent integer values are as decimal, as octal, or as hexadecimal. Octal values are written with a leading 0; hex values are written with a leading 0x. Some valid integers include

```
123
0123
0x123
```

which, of course, in base 10, represent 123, 83, and 291, respectively.

There are four types of integer values, each requiring a different number of bytes of storage: `byte` values hold 1 byte (8 bits); `short` values hold 2 bytes; `int` values hold 4 bytes; and `long` values hold 8 bytes. All values are signed. The maximum and minimum a byte value can hold, for example, are 127 and -128.

You can force a value to be long by appending an *L* (or a lower case *L*) onto the end of the number, which you might need to do for assignments. For example, you can specify a number is defined as `long` by writing:

```
123456789L
```

Performing arithmetic using `byte` and `short` values yields `int` results. If overflow occurs, your number will wrap from the most positive to the most negative value the data type can contain. For example, what if you assign a `byte` variable the value 200? What will the output be? Consider this code:

```
class OverflowExample {
   static public void main(String args[]) {
      System.out.println("byte 200 is " + (byte)200);
   }
}
```

200 is 73 more than the largest allowed value. At 127, add one more and you wrap into negative territory. So, you go from 127 to –128. Now there's 72 more to go—add this to -128, and that's the result. The output from the preceding program is

```
byte 200 is -56
```

What about this next example? What will the output be here?

```
class RoundingExample {
   static public void main(String args[]) {
      System.out.println("int 300.99 is " + (int)300.99);
   }
}
```

Java rounds toward 0 when converting a floating-point value to an integer, so the output is

```
int 300.99 is 300
```

You can cause Java to throw an exception if you do some screwy arithmetic thing in integer math, such as divide by 0 or do a modulo 0. In fact, the compiler won't even let you get away with this if it can help it. Consider Listing 10.3.

Listing 10.3

```
class SomethingScrewy {
   static public void main(String args[]) {
      System.out.println("10/0 is " + 10/0);
   }
}
```

This program results in the following compiler error:

```
SomethingScrewy.java:3: Arithmetic exception.
      System.out.println("10/0 is " + 10/0);
```

If you fake out the compiler, you're on the road to disaster at runtime. Listing 10.4 provides an example:

Listing 10.4

```
class SomethingScrewy {
   static public void main(String args[]) {
      int i = 0;
      System.out.println("10/i is " + 10/i);
   }
}
```

Compiling and running this code results in the following runtime error:

```
java.lang.ArithmeticException / by zero
        at SomethingScrewy.main(SomethingScrewy.java:4)
```

Floating-Point

You can identify your numbers as floating-point values by including a decimal or using an *E* and exponent notation. For example, the following would be considered floating-point values:

```
10.02
1002E-2
1.
```

You can use an *F* (or *f*) to indicate the number is a single-precision floating point number (32 bits) and a *D* (or *d*) to indicate it's a double-precision number (64 bits). For example, you can write

```
1.2F
1.2D
```

for single and double precision, repectively. If you don't specify, the number is double precision.

You can't make assignments that force a value to be coerced in such a way that it loses accuracy. For example, you can assign an int to a float, but you can't assign a float to an int.

Here are some assignments you can make:

```
float   myFloat;
double  myDouble;
int     myInt;
long    myLong;

myFloat = 3;            // Java coerces int to float
myFloat = (float)3;    // explicitly cast an int to a float
myFloat = 3F;          // specify the value as a float
myFloat = (float)1.0;  // cast a double to a float

myDouble = 1.0;        // the default is double precision
myDouble = 1;          // Java coerces int to double
myDouble = 1D;         // specify the value as a double

myInt = (int) 1.0;     // cast double to int
myInt = (int) 1F;      // cast float to int
myInt = (int) 20L;     // cast long to int

myLong = 1;            // Java coerces int to long
myLong = (long) 1.0;   // cast double to long
myLong = (long) 1F;    // cast float to long
```

With floating-point values, you'll never generate an exception when you perform math. This is true even if you divide by 0! An example appears in Listing 10.5.

Listing 10.5

```
class FloatingMath {
    static public void main(String args[]) {
        double d1 = 10.0;
        double d2 = 0.0;
        double d3;
        double d4;

        d3 = d1/d2;
        System.out.println("d3 is " + d3);

        d4 = d3 * 10;
        System.out.println("d4 is " + d4);

    }
}
```

Java maintains a value it refers to as Inf to represent infinity. Here's the output from the program of Listing 10.5:

```
d3 is Inf
d4 is Inf
```

Some infinity math rules include the following:

1. You can have positive and negative infinities.
2. You can't distinguish between infinities of the same sign.
3. If you divide by infinity, you get 0.

Character

In Java, char values are 16-bit Unicode characters. To write out a Unicode character directly, you can use the notation \u*dddd*, where *dddd* are digits.

For example, Listing 10.6 shows some Java code that prints the letter *a*.

Listing 10.6

```
class UnicodeA {
    static public void main(String args[]) {
        String s = new String("\u0061");
        System.out.println(s);
    }
}
```

As with C, you can get some special characters by using the backslash (\). They are listed in Table 10.1. (Note there's no alarm bell with '\a'.)

Boolean

Unlike C/C++, Java reserves the keywords true and false and makes these values part of the language. Booleans must be set to one of these two values; in Java, you can't substitute null or 0 for false or some non-0 amount, like 1, for true. In particular, you cannot convert between a Boolean and a number by casting. If you want to perform a Boolean test, for example, it's not valid to write

Table 10.1 Special characters

Description	Representation	Backslash Sequence
Horizontal tab	HT	\t
Back space	BS	\b
Carriage return	CR	\r
Form feed	FF	\f
Backslash	\	\\
Single quote	'	\'
Double quote	"	\"
Octal bit pattern	Oddd	\ddd
Hex bit pattern	0xdd	\xdd
Unicode char	0xdddd	\udddd

```
MyClass myObject = null;
if (myObject) { // Totally illegal!
}
```

or even

```
int i = 0;
if (i) { // Totally illegal, also!
}
```

Instead, you must make it a Boolean test, such as

```
if (myObject != null) { // Much better!
```

or

```
if (i > 0) { // Now this will work!
```

this, super, and null

We're going to talk about scope next, but before we do, let's cover some details of a few values Java defines that are very useful. You've seen all of these already, but we haven't yet explicitly defined them.

If you don't have an object to refer to at all and want to initialize a variable representing an object to some empty value, you can set the variable to `null`. In general, you can use `null` wherever you might normally use an object in an assignment or as an argument in a parameter list.

As in C++, you can use the variable `this` to refer to the current instance—that is, the instance responding to a method call. `this` is not defined for class methods since there is no current instance in a class method.

Where C++ relies on casting to reference an immediate superclass, in Java you can use a variable called `super`. You can use `super` to pass a call up the ancestor chain if you override methods in subclasses.

Variable Scope

When you refer to a variable, Java goes through a set sequence in finding its value.

First, Java searches for the variable in the current block of code. If the variable name isn't found, Java searches in the block outside that, and so on, up to the beginning of the method.

If the variable isn't found there, Java searches through the current instance variables (if the method that's executing is an instance method, of course).

If it still isn't found, Java will keep on trying by looking through the instance variables in your superclasses. Exasperated but not defeated, Java then searches the other classes in your current package, then the imported classes. Following this, though, Java takes a dive and gives up.

To distinguish between local variables, instance variables defined in the current class, and instance variables you've inherited, you can help Java out either by prefixing your variable with `this` or `super` or by casting the instance to the class where the variable is defined. Listing 10.7 is an example of accessing a local variable, an instance variable, and an inherited variable, all with the same name.

Listing 10.7

```
class BaseClass {
    int i = 100;
    public static void main(String args[]) {
        int i;
        BaseClass base = new BaseClass();
```

```
            DerivedClass derived = new DerivedClass();
            i = 400;

    System.out.println("");
            System.out.println("main for BaseClass");
            System.out.println("i = " + i);
            System.out.println("base.i = " + base.i);
            System.out.println("derived.i = " + derived.i);
            System.out.println("(BaseClass)derived.i = " +
                ((BaseClass)derived).i);
        }
    }

    class DerivedClass extends BaseClass {
        int i = 200;
        DerivedClass() {
            int i;
            i = 300;
            System.out.println("constructor for DerivedClass");
            System.out.println("i is " + i);
            System.out.println("this.i is " + this.i);
            System.out.println("super.i is " + super.i);
        }
    }
```

Here's the output:

```
constructor for DerivedClass
i is 300
this.i is 200
super.i is 100

main for BaseClass
i = 400
base.i = 100
derived.i = 200
(BaseClass)derived.i = 100
```

One more word on scope: You can declare a variable at the beginning of a loop, which can be very convenient, especially if you're prototyping and writing code on the fly. For example, you can write

```
    for (int i = 0; i < 10; i++) {
        // .. refer to i inside the loop, if you'd like to
    }
    // i goes out of scope here!
```

Unlike C++, after the `for` loop ends, `i` goes out of scope, so don't refer to it again unless you redeclare it!

■ OPERATORS

How do you implement algorithms in Java? You use the same kinds of statements you used in your former incarnation as a C/C++ programmer.

Arithmetic Operators

These unary operators

```
~
++      (prefix and postfix)
        (prefix and postfix)
-
```

work just like you're used to in C/C++. The `++` and `--` operators also work with `float` values, adding or subtracting 1.0 as appropriate.

Binary operators are also what you're familiar with. For math, you have

```
+
-
*
/
%
```

Bit Operators

Bit operators include

```
&       (bitwise AND)
|       (bitwise OR)
^       (bitwise XOR)
<<      (left shift)
>>      (sign-propagating right shift)
```

Java defines a new operator to perform another kind of bit operation:

```
>>>     (zero-filled right shift)
```

■ CONTROL FLOW

Using What You Already Know

Before we browse over the control flow statements you have available to you, take note of the following:

1. statement can be a single Java statement or a block of statements defined between brackets {}.

2. Data types (such as boolean) and values can be resolved into these things, as in ($x > 4$) for a Boolean.

3. label means the word at the beginning of a line of code.

Here are the control flow statements:

```
if (boolean) statement
else statement

switch(variable) {
    case value: statements
    default: statements
}

break [label];
continue [label];
return value;
for ([initial value];[end condition];[code executed each
    iteration])
    statement
while (boolean) statement
do statement while(boolean);
label: statement
boolean ? result if true : result if false
```

Although you usually cannot use commas in Java to create compound statements, you can use them inside a for loop construct, as in

```
for (int i = 0, int j = 0; i < 10; i++, j++) {
}
```

There's not much more to say. You already know how to use these control flow statements from C and C++. Java uses them the same way. Have at it!

Using Labels

One difference between Java control flow keywords compared with C and C++ is that Java does not implement `goto` (though Java does reserve `goto` as a keyword). While programmers generally don't use `goto` statements very much, they can still come in handy. This is particularly true when trying to break out of nested loops.

In Java, rather than using a goto to try to achieve this effect, you can use a label. Any statement can have a label. Consider Listing 10.8.

Listing 10.8

```
class LabelExample {
    static public void main(String args[]) {
        int i;
        int j;

outerLoop:
        for (i = 0; i < 3; i++) {
            System.out.println("outer loop index = " + i);
            for (j = 0; j < 3; j++) {
                System.out.println("inner loop index = " + j);
                if (j == 1) {
                    System.out.println("about to break");
                    break;
                }
                System.out.println("did not break");
            }
        }
    }
}
```

Without the `break` statement, of course, we'd see the outer loop go from 0 to 2 and the inner loop go from 0 to 2 with each iteration of the outer loop. With the `break` statement, we get this behavior:

```
outer loop index = 0
inner loop index = 0
did not break
inner loop index = 1
about to break
outer loop index = 1
inner loop index = 0
did not break
inner loop index = 1
about to break
outer loop index = 2
inner loop index = 0
```

```
did not break
inner loop index = 1
about to break
```

That is, it breaks out of the inner loop, falling out to continue with the outer loop.

Now consider Listing 10.9.

Listing 10.9

```
class LabelExample {
    static public void main(String args[]) {
        int i;
        int j;

outerLoop:
        for (i = 0; i < 3; i++) {
            System.out.println("outer loop index = " + i);
            for (j = 0; j < 3; j++) {
                System.out.println("inner loop index = " + j);
                if (j == 1) {
                    System.out.println("about to continue");
                    continue;
                }
                System.out.println("after the continue");
            }
        }
    }
}
```

With a `continue` statement instead of a `break` (and adjusting the printIn messages in the code a little), we get the following:

```
outer loop index = 0
inner loop index = 0
after the continue
inner loop index = 1
about to continue
inner loop index = 2
after the continue
outer loop index = 1
inner loop index = 0
after the continue
inner loop index = 1
about to continue
inner loop index = 2
after the continue
outer loop index = 2
inner loop index = 0
after the continue
```

```
inner loop index = 1
about to continue
inner loop index = 2
after the continue
```

That is, we continue to the next iteration of the inner loop when we hit the `continue` statement.

Now let's use labels for the breaks and continues. Tweaking the code of the first example (Listing 10.8), we use a label and thus halt both loops completely by breaking the outer loop when the inner loop reaches 1. Check out Listing 10.10.

Listing 10.10

```java
class LabelExample {
    static public void main(String args[]) {
        int i;
        int j;

outerLoop:
        for (i = 0; i < 3; i++) {
            System.out.println("outer loop index = " + i);
            for (j = 0; j < 3; j++) {
                System.out.println("inner loop index = " + j);
                if (j == 1) {
                    System.out.println("about to continue");
                    break outerLoop;
                }
                System.out.println("after the continue");
            }
        }
    }
}
```

The output is

```
outer loop index = 0
inner loop index = 0
after the continue
inner loop index = 1
about to continue
```

Adjusting the code of the second example (Listing 10.9) to use a label with the `continue` statement, we get this output:

```
outer loop index = 0
inner loop index = 0
after the continue
inner loop index = 1
about to continue
```

```
outer loop index = 1
inner loop index = 0
after the continue
inner loop index = 1
about to continue
outer loop index = 2
inner loop index = 0
after the continue
inner loop index = 1
about to continue
```

That is, we loop through the outer loop 3 times, as expected, but we break out of the inner loop whenever the loop index reaches 1.

■ PROTOTYPING (PART 2)

Let's get back to the Einstein application. When we last tuned in, we had defined the application's class interfaces and set up the application's architecture. It's as if we used a lead pencil to sketch an outline for a picture. Now it's time to use our colored pencils and fill it in.

First of all, what is the calculation we're performing? Special relativity works like this: When observers are moving in relation to one another, they will experience events differently. (Get it? Special relativity. And you thought this concept was difficult.) This is true because measurements of time and space are not absolute but are measured relative to other frames of reference. In our everyday world, the effects of special relativity are very small. However, things become especially interesting as one observer starts moving at speeds close to the speed of light relative to another observer. Then they *really* start experiencing things differently!

One of the most interesting effects of moving near the speed of light is that for the speedy traveler, relative to a stationary traveler, time slows down. That is, while neither traveler will experience time passing any differently than is normal, their pocket watches will tick at different speeds. Just how differently is provided in this equation:

■ t = distance/velocity * square root[1 – (velocity/C)2]

Less compactly, in English,

■ The time that elapses is equal to (the distance traveled divided by the speed of travel) times the square root of (one minus the fraction of the speed of light being traveled, squared).

You can see, from this formula, why speeds greater than the speed of light are not allowed. In those cases, velocity/C will be greater than 1, and we'd be taking the square root of a negative number.

Let's start by implementing this formula in Java. We're going to have our SpaceShip class handle this time dilation calculation. Given the distance we want to travel, in light-years, and given that this SpaceShip instance keeps track of the user's speed, here's the method:

```
double calcTimeDilation(double distanceLightYr)
   throws WarpException {

   double distanceKm = Light.lightYearToKm(distanceLightYr);
   if (fraction > 1.0)
      throw new WarpException();

   return (distanceKm/speed) * Math.sqrt(1.0 -
      (fraction*fraction));
}
```

We use the public `sqrt()` method that's in the Math class. Since floating-point arithmetic will never throw an exception, we first check to see whether the user has entered a value that indicates we're going faster than light. If so, we throw the exception we've defined to indicate we're entering warp speed. Also, to make the units come out right, we have to convert the distance we're traveling to a distance in kilometers rather than light-years. We've defined a utility to handle this called `lightYearToKm()` that we keep in the Light class. (Note that both `speed` and `fraction` are instance variables for SpaceShip.)

Let's implement our `main()` method so that it performs the following five tasks:

1. Tells the user what's going on.
2. Asks for input.
3. Acquires any other data necessary to calculate the time dilation (in particular, the distance being traveled).
4. Performs its calculations.
5. Shows the user the results.

Here's the beginning of our `main()` routine:

```
Galaxy      destination = new Andromeda();
double      distanceLightYears = destination.getDistance();
SpaceShip   enterprise;
double      time;

showInstructions();
enterprise = new SpaceShip(getPercentC());
time = enterprise.calcTimeDilation(distanceLightYears);
showResults(time);
```

Now, let's add to this outline a little. We want to show what's going on back on earth for our stationary observer:

```
showBackOnEarth(distanceLightYears, enterprise.speed);
```

To determine how much time has elapsed on earth, we need to know how far we're traveling and how fast, so we pass in this information in the method's parameter list.

Also, remember, we might have thrown a `WarpException` in the time dilation calculation! So, let's handle that here:

```
try {
    // ... the preceding code for main() ...
} catch (WarpException e) {
    System.out.println("Sorry, dilithium crystals have not
been discovered yet.");
```

In addition to our own, a number of other exceptions might occur along the way. These include I/O and conversion errors between the characters the user entered and the floating-point number we want. So, let's be prepared to catch all the other possible exceptions as well:

```
} catch (Exception e) {
    // ... handle any errors if we want to ...
}
```

Getting input from the user is similar to what you've already seen in the first Quick Start chapter. We keep on reading from the input stream until we notice the user has hit the carriage return. Then, we take those characters and convert them into a double data type, using methods available from the Double wrapper class. Also, since we might throw an exception, we have to indicate that we do not handle it in this method:

```
static double getPercentC()
      throws java.io.IOException {
   StringBuffer buffer = new StringBuffer();
   char          c;

   while ((c = (char)System.in.read()) != '\n')
      buffer.append(c);

   return Double.valueOf(buffer.toString()).doubleValue();
}
```

We create a SpaceShip instance when the user enters the ship's speed as a percentage of the speed of light. Since the SpaceShip instance needs to know the speed it's traveling for the time dilation calculation in addition to the fraction of the speed of light, it's convenient to keep track of both of these values as part of the SpaceShip instance so that they're always available:

```
double fraction;      // fraction of the speed of light
double speed;         // speed in km/yr

SpaceShip(double percent) {
   fraction = percent/100.0;
   speed = fraction * Light.Ckm_yr;
}
```

We use the Light class to maintain the speed of light in the units kilometers per year in addition to meters per second.

Also, recall that we only defined an abstract class called Galaxy that was to be the superclass for our various long-range destinations. So, we define a particular example of a Galaxy—namely, Andromeda—to be a subclass and implement the abstract methods it inherits:

```
abstract class Galaxy {
   abstract public double getDistance();
}

class Andromeda extends Galaxy {
   public double getDistance() {
      return 2.2E6; // in light-years
   }
}
```

The complete source code for the Einstein application is listed in Appendix B.

Here are some examples of running this application. (The bold-faced values are the sample values entered.)

What if we travel at 90% of the speed of light?

```
Enter your speed as a percentage of the speed of
light. I will calculate the time required for you to travel
to the Andromeda galaxy, 2.2 million light-years away.

90
Travel time as you perceive it,
with relativistic effects, is:
1065508 years and 230 days.

Back on earth, 2444444 years and
162 days would have elapsed.
```

Egad! Traveling at 90% of the speed of light, we'd get to Andromeda in about 1-million years as far as our on-board clock is concerned. However, back on earth, 2.4-million years would have elapsed.

What if we push it and get up to 99% of the speed of light?

```
Enter your speed as a percentage of the speed of
light. I will calculate the time required for you to travel
to the Andromeda galaxy, 2.2 million light-years away.

99
Travel time as you perceive it,
with relativistic effects, is:
313483 years and 7 days.

Back on earth, 2222222 years and
81 days would have elapsed.
```

We'd get there faster, but the trip would still take too long. As it happens, we have to travel *really, really* fast to reach Andromeda in our lifetime.

Try entering 99.99999999, for example (99 followed by eight 9s). You'll get the following:

```
99.99999999
Travel time as you perceive it,
with relativistic effects, is:
31 years and 41 days.
```

```
Back on earth, 2200000 years and
0 days would have elapsed.
```

At so close to the speed of light, the elapsed time on earth is essentially the time it takes light to reach Andromeda—2.2-million years. However, time slows down enough for you to still be alive if you exercise and eat right along the way.

You can also enter 100% and get there in no time (literally, as far as you're concerned) but 2.2-million years would have slipped by on earth.

■ SUMMARY

This chapter showed you the details of implementing a class. We also completed the Einstein application by filling in the outline we started in the previous chapter.

Many of the constructs you've come to know and love in C and C++ are available in Java as well. These include the arithmetic and bit operators and lots of the flow control statements. Java tosses in a new operator for shifting right and the ability to break and continue using labels to identify lines of code.

■ WHAT'S NEXT?

You've learned all the basics of the Java language, but there are a handful of advanced topics awaiting. These include arrays, strings, multitasking, and exceptions. The next chapter pokes into these topics to round out your knowledge of what the Java language has to offer. After that, we'll mop up the remaining nooks and crannies of the language by looking at work-arounds for items removed from C++, and you'll see how to optimize your code. Then, it's time for the libraries!

11

More Power to You

Chapter 11 shows you how to take advantage of some of Java's more advanced features, such as threads and exceptions. It also illustrates some subtle changes to common data types you're very familiar with from C/C++—in particular, changes to arrays and strings to make them first-class objects. Now that we've toured the universe in the previous chapters, we'll shift gears and look at a couple of more down-to-earth examples: a simulation of a pendulum and a visit to a local town hall meeting.

■ ARRAYS

Arrays in C/C++

In C and C++, an array declaration such as

```
int arr[1000];
```

sets aside a block of memory large enough to hold 1,000 integers. You can start using this memory immediately, and directly, to store and retrieve integers. Since the memory is defined at compile time, the array must be defined using a constant. That is, you can't use a variable that you initialize at runtime to specify the length of the array. (You can, of course, use `malloc()`, as discussed later.)

So far, all is well and fine. The sticky part about arrays comes into play with the fact that C and C++ treat arrays and pointers as essentially similar things. That is, with the example array declaration just given, `arr` is equivalent to `&arr[0]`. By definition, `arr + 1` is equal to `&arr[1]`, and `*(arr + 1)` is `arr[1]`. This is all very cool and very powerful in C/C++. It's how things are done in C, though it can be confusing.

Unfortunately, you can get yourself into lots of trouble. In particular, there's nothing in the language that stops you from accessing element `arr[1000]` even though the last element in this block of memory is located at `arr[999]`. What's more, there's nothing that stops you from *writing* to this location. Gadzooks! Here's an example of how to allow memory to get squashed that you might easily overlook in your code:

```
#include <iostream.h>
main () {
    char name[20];
    int veryImportantNumber = 123;
    cin >> name;
}
```

This program runs fine until George Washington Carver tries to enter his name. At this point, our `veryImportantNumber`, if the compiler set aside this memory right after `name[20]`, gets stomped on. The point is not that C and C++ are inherently dangerous (even if they are); the point is that *you* have to keep tabs on the memory. You have to remember how memory is laid out in your application so that other pieces of your code don't come along and do things they shouldn't.

This also brings up an even more subtle problem that is part of C++. It's not enough just to avoid accessing memory beyond the bounds of your array. When you delete the array, you also need to remember to tell the system that the memory you're referring to is actually an array and not simply the first element of the array.

For example, you could write a program in C++ like this:

```
class MyClass {
}

main () {
  MyClass *mc = new MyClass[3];
  delete mc;
}
```

This program would cause only `mc[0]` to be deleted, resulting in a memory leak. Try executing this as part of your payroll processing, creating and deleting thousands of arrays incorrectly, and you'll get paged in the middle of the night when your program stops working because it ran out of memory and the Very Big Company, Inc., wants to know who the programmer was. Rather than living this nightmare, always remember the data types you're dealing with and, when dealing with arrays of objects, instead write

```
delete [] mc;
```

These are examples of either not accessing memory you're supposed to access, or not allocating enough memory, or not freeing enough memory. In all three cases, your program will keep on chugging along until, at some point, either 1 nanosecond later or many days in the future, your program will crash and burn, and you're likely to have no idea why. In Java, this problem *never* occurs.

Arrays in Java

Arrays in Java are first-class objects that have a public instance variable called `length`. As with arrays in C/C++, you can use pretty much the same syntax to access elements from arrays:

```
myElement = myArray[nthEntry];
```

Since arrays are 0 based, as they are in C/C++, accessing `myArray[0]` gets the first element, `myArray[1]` gets the second, and so on. But keep in mind that myArray is not a pointer (there aren't any pointers in Java). So, even though the syntax is familiar, don't try to perform pointer arithmetic, such as trying to access `*(myArray+1)`.

When you access an array, Java checks the subscripts you use. You'll never have to worry about mangling memory by writing beyond the bounds of the array or about reading garbage data by reading outside the array's bounds. However, if you do try to access an element that's beyond the bounds of the array, you'll cause Java to throw an exception called `ArrayIndexOutOfBoundsException`, which will stop your program if you don't catch it. In other words, rather than allowing you to access memory you shouldn't, Java slams the door in your face. So, as with C and C++, use good programming practice so that your program executes as you intend.

Arrays can be allocated using this format:

```
<type> <name>[] = new <type>[<length>]
```

For example, you can allocate an array of 127 characters like this:

```
char myCharArray[] = new char[127];
```

So, you're asking, if arrays are first-class objects, what's the data type that indicates this? We're using `char` to indicate both a simple data type and a first-class array object. The key is this: Java uses the preceding notation to keep things familiar to C/C++ programmers. However, the `char` array class can also be written like this:

```
char[]
```

This notation helps make it clear what data type you're dealing with. That is, if you define

```
char[] myCharArray;
```

there's no doubt you're dealing with an object that represents an array of characters. This notation is used in the rest of this book.

When you define an array's length, you can use any integer. So,

```
int i = 3;
char[] name = new char[i];
```

works just as well as

```
char[] name = new char[3];
```

Another nice thing about arrays in Java is that the memory is initialized for you. You don't have to immediately go into a loop setting the elements in an array of objects, for example, to null or the values in an array of Booleans to false. Java automatically initializes all array elements to 0, null, or false, as appropriate.

Arrays and the Data Types They Represent

Implicit for each simple data type is an array object. That is, there's an array object for int, short, char, float, and so on. Java's class libraries also implicitly define arrays representing each of the classes they define.

The same is true with classes you define yourself That is, Java defines an array data type for each of your own classes. The elements of the array object are automatically large enough to contain the objects to which they refer. So, for example, if you have a class called Eagle, you can define and allocate an Eagle array like this:

```
Eagle[] e = new Eagle[3];
```

Arrays connect up to the class hierarchy separately from the objects that make up their elements. That is, if Bird descends from Animal, then Bird[] descends from Animal[], and the objects Bird and Bird[] are siblings. Similarly, if Eagle descends from class Bird, then Eagle[] descends from Bird[]. But keep in mind all this "array as a class" stuff is implicit. For example, you cannot directly subclass Eagle[].

Arrays of Arrays

If you're working in C and you're creating an application that simulates a Little League baseball scorecard, you might define a two-dimensional array like this:

```
char scorecard[14][9];
```

You've defined enough rows for each team to bat for 7 innings and enough columns for the team to send each player to the plate. Or have you?

What happens in a rally, where a team sends more than 9 players to the plate? In that case, you don't have enough memory allocated to record what happens in the game. (Since there are no extra innings in Little League, 14 rows is enough. If you wanted to allow extra innings, this problem would have to be overcome as well using the same technique described in this section.)

In C, you might try the following technique. You begin by defining the 14 rows for your scorecard. However, you don't yet specify how long each row should be. Instead, you leave that open-ended:

```
char scorecard[14][];
```

What you have in C, then, is essentially an array of pointers (Figure 11.1).

In particular, you have an array that will contain arrays. Now, after the top of the first, you can allocate enough memory to store what occurred for each batter, and you can assign that memory to the first element in the scorecard array:

```
// C code to allocate columns one at a time
*halfInning = malloc(numBatters * sizeof(char));
scorecard[1][] = halfInning;
```

Figure 11.1   An array of pointers in C

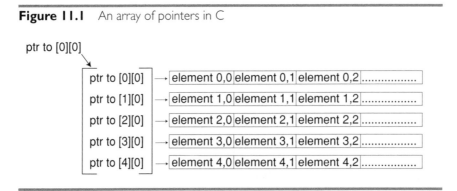

While this program is extremely flexible, you have programmed your way into a huge memory management burden. Now your arrays are of variable length. You must be sure to pass this multidimensional array around your program correctly, and, at some point, when you need to free this array of pointers, you'll have to do so very carefully to ensure the correct amount of memory is recycled.

With Java, you can also have an array of arrays. And, since Java manages the memory, you never run into the difficulties that you run into with C. In fact, not only can you have multidimensional arrays such as

```
int[][]
```

but also you can define Rubik's cubes (or any dimension array you'd like to) like this:

```
int[][][]
```

Returning to a two-dimensional array, remember that you don't have to allocate the memory for an instance when you first declare it. So, you can write

```
char[][] scorecard = new char[14][];
```

At this point, you've defined an array of arrays. When you need to record the batters for a particular half-inning, you can write

```
scorecard[0] = new char[numBatters];
```

and assign each element in your array their scorecard codes, such as

```
scorecard[0][0] = '1'; // single
scorecard[0][1] = 'o'; // strikeout (goose egg)
scorecard[0][2] = 'g'; // groundout
```

and so on. You can obtain the lengths of these arrays at any time. You can get the number of rows like this:

```
scorecard.length
```

This would yield 14 in this example. You can access the number of columns for a row (such as for the first one) like this:

```
scorecard[0].length
```

This would be equal to whatever the original value is for `numBatters`.

Don't try to access an element of an array until you have allocated it. For example, without assigning something to `scorecard[1]`, you'd receive a `NullPointerException` if you tried to obtain its length, as in

```
scorecard[1].length
```

To avoid this kind of exception, you can check first to see whether this element in the array is allocated:

```
if (scorecard[1] != null) {
    // ... your code here ...
}
```

Arrays as Data Types

You can check to see whether an array is an instance of a certain type of array. Listing 11.1 shows an example of using `instanceof` with an array type.

Listing 11.1

```
class ClassTester {
  static public void main(String args[]) {
    Eagle e = new Eagle();
    Eagle[] eArr = new Eagle[3];

    System.out.println("Eagle object:");
    testObject(e);
    testEagle(e);
    testObjectArray(e);
    testEagleArray(e);

    System.out.println("\nEagle array object:");
    testObject(eArr);
    testEagle(eArr);
    testObjectArray(eArr);
    testEagleArray(eArr);
  }

  static void testObject(Object o) {
    System.out.println("Object? " + (o instanceof Object));
  }

  static void testEagle(Object o) {
    System.out.println("Eagle? " + (o instanceof Eagle));
  }

  static void testObjectArray(Object o) {
    System.out.println("ObjectArray? " + (o instanceof Object[]));
  }
```

```
    static void testEagleArray(Object o) {
      System.out.println("EagleArray? " + (o instanceof Eagle[]));
    }
}
```

The output for this little class is

```
Eagle object:
Object? true
Eagle? true
ObjectArray? false
EagleArray? false

Eagle array object:
Object? true
Eagle? false
ObjectArray? true
EagleArray? true
```

Casting Arrays

Since the implicit array classes descend from class Object, you can cast between objects and arrays by widening and narrowing, just as you would cast other objects. For example, you can cast an array to an object (narrowing) and cast an object to a particular type of array (widening). Listing 11.2 illustrates casting between arrays and objects.

Listing 11.2

```
class Caster {
    static public void main(String[] args) {
      int[]  a = new int[3];
      Object o;

      o = a;         // int[] descends from class Object.
      a = (int[])o; // o refers to an array (we just assigned it)
    }
}
```

■ STRINGS

Strings in C/C++

In C and C++, strings are implemented as character arrays. The C/C++ libraries provide all sorts of powerful functions you can use to manipulate strings. Because strings are arrays, they allow all the same techniques for manipulating memory—namely, pointer arithmetic—with their inherent powers and lurking dangers.

Using the String Class in Java

In Java, you can still create an array of characters. However, if you want to use text, it's much more convenient to use the String and StringBuffer classes instead.

Before we turn to String and StringBuffer, let's first look at character arrays. You can declare the length of an array and initialize the array at the same time by using notation similar to that in C/C++:

```
char[] c = {'a', 'b', 'c'};
```

You can also declare and initialize a character array one element at a time:

```
char[] c = new char[3];
c[0] = 'a';
c[1] = 'b';
c[2] = 'c';
```

Note that, while arrays are convenient for dealing with collections of data, they don't know a whole lot about manipulating text. In addition, 1-byte characters are not good for internationalization.

Instead of a character array, you could use a String or StringBuffer object to store text. For example, you can define a new String object like this:

```
String s = new String("Caffeine is good");
```

Java also defines a kind of shorthand notation for declaring and initializing strings:

```
String s = "Caffeine is good";
```

In using either notation, you don't have to worry about counting out the letters, making sure your char array is big enough, and so on. In addition, there are lots of String methods for working with individual characters.

Strings also use 2 bytes to store each character so that they can take advantage of Unicode. This makes it possible to write software in any language (which could be particularly important in the borderless Web).

Reading and Writing Strings

String is read-only; StringBuffer is read and write. One does not descend from the other, so you must be certain to use the correct object type when required in calling sequences and so on. To get a String from a String-Buffer, you can use the StringBuffer method `toString()`, as in

```
StringBuffer sb = new StringBuffer("hey there");
String s = sb.toString();
```

Although String and StringBuffer are defined similarly, when you define a String, you must initialize it at the time it is created. String-Buffer instances require more system overhead but can be appended to or modified at any time. To accept input, for example, you'll use a StringBuffer, as in

```
char    c;
StringBuffer  strng;

while ((c = (char)System.in.read()) != -1)
      strng.appendChar(c);
```

which reads from the standard input until the end-of-data indicator comes across (such as command-Z).

Manipulating Strings

String and StringBuffer objects sport the only example of operator over-loading that exists in Java. As you've seen in various examples through this book, you can use the + operator to append to a String or String-Buffer. For example, you can write

```
StringBuffer a = new StringBuffer("Now is ");
a = a + "the time...";
```

Strings also can take the + operator when they're first created, as in

```
String s = new String("Four score and " + "seven years ago...");
```

By the way, += is not overloaded, so you cannot append to a String-Buffer using this notation.

There are quite a few methods that String defines for accessing pieces of a string. For example, charAt() will return a character at a particular location; getChars() and substring() will return pieces of a String; and replace() will replace a particular character with another one through the length of the String. Java's class libraries describe the methods available to you in detail.

■ MULTITASKING

A Possible C/C++ Approach

Though it is possible to implement multitasking on almost any platform using C or C++, there are two major hurdles to overcome:

1. Your implementation is likely to be very platform dependent.
2. You will probably have to manage all the interprocess communication and synchronization yourself.

A possible approach in Unix is to make a system call to fork a process or start a new one. You could then use Remote Procedure Calls to communicate between applications.

However, this approach does not even begin to address synchronization problems such as the dueling teller machines predicament described in Part I. If you use class libraries that provide multitasking, you still run into the wall of platform dependence.

Multitasking in Java

In Java, implementing multitasking is not an operating system hack. It's part of the language and class packages.

Here's the basis of what happens: There is a class called `Thread` that runs as a lightweight process. To coordinate among different threads, you can use locks. One lock is associated with an object, and one lock is associated with its class. If you call an instance method that you've indicated can be executed only by one thread at a time, the called object's lock is used to block access to that method until that method exits (and so automatically releases the lock). The class lock is used with static methods.

You can get multiple threads to weave all through your system simply by instantiating the Thread class or derived classes and starting these instances on their merry ways. Keywords that you specify help Java figure out when and how to coordinate among threads.

Threads

You can create a new Thread object just as you would any other object:

```
Thread t = new Thread();
```

To start the thread, you call its `start()` method:

```
t.start();
```

This call creates the system resources required to run a new thread and makes Java call the thread's `run()` method. The thread will live as long as the `run()` method does not exit and as long as no one calls `stop()` on the thread.

When the thread does stop, its `stop()` method gets called. You can subclass and override any of these three methods to perform your own initialization, run instructions, and clean up. At a minimum, you must override `run()` or your thread won't have any real purpose in life.

Listing 11.3 gives an example of a simple thread. All this Thread subclass does is override its `run()` method to show you that it is indeed working.

Listing 11.3

```
class MyClass {
    public static void main(String args[]) {
```

```
        MyThread t = new MyThread();
        t.start();
    }
}

class MyThread extends Thread {
    public void run() {
        System.out.println("running...");
    }
}
```

The output from this program is simply

```
running...
```

Let's look at a more involved example by checking out what occurs in a town hall meeting. If you've never been to one, you're about to experience such a meeting in all its glory.

First the emcee (MC) gets up and says hello. Then, any speakers that have something to say step up to the podium and speak. The town hall meeting is run in such a way that everyone speaks their mind and no utterance gets lost in the rush to make a case. The emcee allows statements to be heard one at a time. After everyone has said his or her piece and no other speakers are waiting to say something, the emcee says goodnight, the good citizens leave, and the town hall closes.

We have a number of actors in this play: an emcee and some speakers. Since each of these participants is an individual, we can model each as an individual thread. (However, we will need to provide coordination among them; we'll get to that shortly.)

Here's how we can begin to define the participants (the complete source is in Appendix B):

```
class Speaker extends Thread {
        int              id;
        int              speech_count;
        SynchronizedQueue my_soapbox;

        Speaker(int new_id, int turns, SynchronizedQueue forum) {
                id = new_id;
                speech_count = turns;
                my_soapbox = forum;
        }
}
```

```
class MC extends Thread {
        SynchronizedQueue podium;
        MC(SynchronizedQueue new_forum) {
                podium = new_forum;
        }
}
```

Speakers wear a name tag (an `id`). They also arrive with a certain number of points to make (a `speech_count`). They know where they're going to deliver their wisdom (on `my_soapbox`). The emcee only needs to know where the podium is. Also referred to here is a new class, SynchronizedQueue (which is explained momentarily).

Let's create five speakers at this town hall meeting. We'll enlist the help of a famous political pundit/moderator to assist with our little gathering and assign him the role of emcee:

```
int num_speakers = 5;

Speaker[] contenders = new Speaker[num_speakers];
MC georgeWill = new MC(podium);

georgeWill.start();

for(int i = 0; i < num_speakers; i++) {
        contenders[i] = new Speaker(i, 10, podium);
        contenders[i].start();
}
```

Notice that for each new Thread we create, we must initiate it by calling its `start()` method. Until we do, it won't actually be doing anything. The Thread instance will exist in memory, but no system resources will be allocated to it to allow it to run as a separate process.

Now let's deal with SynchronizedQueue. The podium will be a subclass we'll create that is a kind of magical and very fair podium: When a speaker says something, the podium will ensure that the speaker's message does not overlay someone else's message and squash that person's equally precious two cents. How this occurs is described in a few moments.

Here's the outline for our podium subclass:

```
class SynchronizedQueue extends Vector {

        private int     count;
        private boolean started;
```

```
SynchronizedQueue() {
        count = 0;
        started = false;
    }
}
```

As you can see from the class definition, the podium knows how many messages are waiting to be said and whether people have started speaking yet.

So what gets said? At this town hall, the citizens are up in arms. There are quite a number of issues on their minds, and they don't hesitate to say them! These issues range from banning monkeys to selling computers, from importing books to outlawing bicycles. Here's a sample town hall session:

```
MC here: good morning.
speaker 4 stepping onto soapbox
speaker 1 stepping onto soapbox
speaker 3 stepping onto soapbox
speaker 0 stepping onto soapbox
speaker 0: music should be bought
speaker 2 stepping onto soapbox
speaker 1: bicycles should be given away
speaker 3: bicycles should be given away
speaker 4: music should be bought
speaker 2: bicycles should be given away
speaker 1: cars should be bought
speaker 2: cars should be bought
speaker 1: dogs should be exported
speaker 1: elephants should be outlawed
speaker 0: dogs should be banned
speaker 0: music should be deported
speaker 3: cars should be bought
speaker 3: dogs should be exported
speaker 3: elephants should be outlawed
speaker 0: monkeys should be imported
speaker 0: donkeys should be sold
speaker 0: books should be made mandatory
speaker 0: music should be made mandatory
speaker 0: bicycles should be encouraged
speaker 4: dogs should be banned
speaker 4: music should be deported
speaker 3: cars should be given away
speaker 3: cars should be made mandatory
speaker 2: dogs should be exported
speaker 1: cars should be given away
speaker 0: dogs should be given away
speaker 4: monkeys should be imported
speaker 1: cars should be made mandatory
speaker 4: donkeys should be sold
```

```
speaker 2: elephants should be outlawed
speaker 2: cars should be given away
speaker 4: books should be made mandatory
speaker 3: houses should be given away
speaker 1: houses should be given away
speaker 1: books should be imported
speaker 0: donkeys should be discouraged
speaker 1: music should be made mandatory
speaker 1: dogs should be made mandatory
speaker 1 stepping off soapbox
speaker 2: cars should be made mandatory
speaker 3: books should be imported
speaker 4: music should be made mandatory
speaker 0 stepping off soapbox
speaker 4: bicycles should be encouraged
speaker 4: dogs should be given away
speaker 3: music should be made mandatory
speaker 2: houses should be given away
speaker 2: books should be imported
speaker 4: donkeys should be discouraged
speaker 4 stepping off soapbox
speaker 3: dogs should be made mandatory
speaker 3 stepping off soapbox
speaker 2: music should be made mandatory
speaker 2: dogs should be made mandatory
speaker 2 stepping off soapbox
MC here: good night.
Town Hall closing.
```

Why do the good citizens say such things? Well, they only know what they read in the local paper, and everything they read is sorted into nouns and actions and gets stored in their minds. Here's what the speakers' warehouse of activist thoughts looks like:

```
static String nouns[] = {
        "dogs", "cats", "elephants", "donkeys", "houses",
        "monkeys", "cars", "bicycles", "computers",
        "music", "books" };

static String ends[] = {
        "outlawed", "banned", "imported", "discouraged",
        "sold", "bought", "given away", "made mandatory",
        "encouraged", "deported", "exported" };
```

When speakers say something, they randomly connect a noun to an action. This activity occurs as follows:

```
public void run() {
    int i;
    Random r = new Random();
```

```
my_soapbox.checkIn();
my_soapbox.enqueue("speaker "+ id +" stepping onto soapbox");

for (i = 0; i < speech_count; i++) {
   my_soapbox.enqueue("speaker "+ id +": " +
   nouns[Math.abs(r.nextInt())%nouns.length] + " should be " +
      ends[Math.abs(r.nextInt())%ends.length]);
}

my_soapbox.enqueue("speaker "+ id +" stepping off soapbox");
my_soapbox.checkOut();
}
```

That is, a speaker checks in at the town hall, steps up to the soapbox, randomly holds forth on what that speaker has read about, and then steps off the soapbox and checks out. The speakers' utterances are not heard by the audience right away. The emcee, as you'll see, helps ensure their statements are heard one at a time.

The Life Cycle of a Thread

Threads have definite life cycles. Depending on where a thread is in its life cycle, it can be in one of a number of states.

New thread—When you create a new thread object, it's raring to go, but until you call its `start()` method, it's just a new thread without a life.

Runnable—Once you call `start()`, the thread executes its `start()` method and calls `run()`. If someone calls `stop()` on the thread or if the `run()` method exits, the thread will transition to *dead*. The thread will remain runnable, even if it's not the highest-priority thread and so is not actually currently running. A thread can, however, drop out of the runnable state and become not runnable.

Not runnable—A thread can become runnable again, but it can also be killed while in this state if someone calls the thread's `stop()` method.

Dead—Once a thread dies, it's just waiting to be garbage-collected and can't be resuscitated.

A thread can transition in and out of the runnable state during its life in a number of ways.

Someone could call the thread's `suspend()` method. If this occurs, the thread will be restarted only if someone calls its `resume()` method at some later time.

Someone could halt the thread for a specified number of milliseconds using its `sleep()` method. The thread will start up again automatically (if its priority is the highest) after the specified number of milliseconds have elapsed.

The thread itself could call `wait()`. To get a waiting thread going again, you can use the method `notify()` or `notifyAll()`. This wakes up the thread.

The thread could be blocked by another thread that is hogging I/O. If a thread B were trying to read from the keyboard at the same time the user is typing in some data in response to a thread A, thread B would just have to wait. Once the I/O was free again, thread B would continue on. (To be safer, you can also wrap your I/O in a synchronized method.)

For the town hall meeting, the emcee allows utterances to be heard by taking them from the podium one at a time. To do this, the podium's `dequeue()` method is invoked. Once all the utterances have been heard by the audience, the emcee says good night. At that point, the emcee's thread comes to an end. Here's what the `run()` method for the emcee looks like:

```java
public void run() {
        Object utterance;

        System.out.println("MC here: good morning.");

        utterance = podium.dequeue();
        while (utterance != null) {
                System.out.println(utterance);
                utterance = podium.dequeue();
        }

        System.out.println("MC here: good night.");
}
```

So how does the podium dequeue the statements when the emcee retrieves them? First, the podium makes sure there are speakers left. If there are, but there is currently nothing to be said, the podium waits:

```
while (anyoneLeft() && (super.elementCount == 0)) {
        try {
                wait();
        } catch (InterruptedException x) { }
}
```

Here, the thread goes to sleep when it calls `wait()`. Everytime it's awakened, it checks to see whether the conditions that put it to sleep have changed. As you now know, when a thread calls `wait()`, the only way it can continue is to get notified that something has changed. In particular, the thread should be notified:

- either when a speaker checks out
- or when a speaker says something

If a speaker checks out, then there might not be any speakers left, so we might not have anything more to wait for. If a speaker says something, then we can dequeue that utterance and pass it back to the emcee to be heard. So, SynchronizedQueue makes sure it issues a `notify()` in both of these situations:

```
public synchronized void checkOut () {
        count--;
        notify();
}

public synchronized void enqueue(Object elt) {
        super.addElement(elt);
        notify();
}
```

Let's take a look at the `synchronized` keyword next.

Synchronization and Monitors

Chapter 3 covered the concepts concerning synchronization. Here's an example of why it might be bad *not* to synchronize in the town hall application. The application adds an utterance to the queue by calling the queue's `addElement()` method:

```
super.addElement(elt);
```

We, as the consumers of this class package, do not know how the method `addElement()` is implemented. It might, for example, be implemented as five separate operations:

1. Fetch the queue.
2. Create a new queue that is one element longer.
3. Copy the elements from the old queue to the new queue.
4. Add the new element to the new queue.
5. Replace the old queue with the new queue.

Now, certainly, this might not be the most efficient way to go, but the point is that calling `addElement()` is not necessarily one machine instruction. Any number of things could be occurring within this call.

What would happen if speaker 1 added an element and got as far as step 4 in the list just given when speaker 2, running as a separate thread, preempts to add an utterance? If speaker 2 made it through all five steps before speaker 1 was allowed to continue, speaker 1 would overwrite the queue and speaker 2's utterance would never be heard by the audience.

To stop speaker 2's comments from becoming lost in the sands of time, we can indicate that only one speaker can add comments to the queue at any one time. We declare the method to be `synchronized`.

```
public synchronized void enqueue(Object elt) {
```

How does Java perform this synchronization? Java associates a monitor with each object and with each class. When a thread enters a synchronized method, that thread enters the appropriate monitor as well. When the thread exits the synchronized method, it also exits the monitor. In the preceding example, Java uses the monitor associated with the instance since this is an instance method. If this were a static method, Java would use the monitor associated with the class.

Once you call a synchronized method, any other call to a synchronized method for that instance must wait until the thread exits the monitor. The important concept to grasp here is that Java is performing this synchronization as part of the language. Java is handling all the bookkeeping; all you have to do is use the correct keyword.

Note that a thread exits the monitor for a synchronized method when it calls `wait()`, as in the example given earlier. Exiting the monitor gives other threads a chance to change the conditions the first thread is waiting on.

Avoiding Deadlock

One tricky logic problem that Java can't always help you avoid is deadlock. It sounds painful, and it is. Specifically, deadlock occurs if more than one thread is running, and each is attempting to access a locked resource guarded by the other.

For example, imagine if the town hall application were implemented a different way. What if a speaker would say something only if that person could step up to an empty podium, and what if the emcee was on the podium waiting for a speaker to step up before the emcee stepped off? Figure 11.2 portrays the situation.

Java does try to eliminate deadlock situations it can detect. For example, what happens if you implement a recursive algorithm for a synchronized method? Consider Listing 11.4.

Listing 11.4

```
class Factorial {
    static public void main(String[] args) {
        Factorial f = new Factorial();
        int result = f.calculate(10);
    }
    synchronized int calculate(int number) {
        if (number == 1)
            return 1;
        else
            return calculate(number - 1) * number;
    }
}
```

What's the result of this program? Do we hit a deadlock condition because we lock the instance's monitor with the first call to `calculate()`, and then wait forever in the recursive call to `calculate(number - 1)` because we're still inside `calculate()`?

Figure 11.2   Deadlock with polite town hall participants

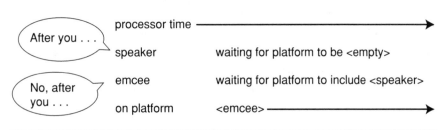

Amazingly, no. Java knows enough to allow the reentry to occur. The secret is that once a thread obtains the lock, it does not have to obtain it again, so recursion is possible for synchronized methods. This program will work just fine.

To help avoid deadlock situations, you should try not to execute one synchronized method from within another synchronized method. If you can do this, you'll never run into trouble. But if this can't be helped, you should at least try to only use a monitor for the shortest amount of time. In particular, try not to lock a method that does something that might take a long time, such as performing a lengthy calculation, writing data to a printer, or accessing files over a network.

To help cut down the amount of time you need to create a lock, you can lock particular blocks of code rather than entire methods. For that, you use the synchronized statement. You specify the lock you'd like to use in this statement, which can be either a particular instance or a class. For example, to use a class's monitor as a lock, use the synchronized statement like this:

```
synchronized (MyClass) {
    // ... your locked code goes here
}
```

Or, to use an instance, supply the instance in this statement:

```
synchronized (myObject) {
    // ... your locked code goes here
}
```

When the synchronized block exits or wait() is called, the lock is released.

Priorities

With more than one thing happening at once—that is, with more than one thread—how does Java provide coordination among threads? Java uses a fixed-priority scheduling algorithm. That is, threads are scheduled based on their priorities. The highest-priority thread is always the one that's running. If there's more than one thread with the same highest-priority, Java has the ability to switch between them. Java can perform preemptive multitasking. In particular, the highest priority thread will always be the one that runs. For example, if a lower-priority thread suddenly becomes a higher-priority thread, the other thread will be suspended, and the new, higher-priority thread will start executing immediately.

A thread can also yield to other threads that have the same priority as itself (or to new or existing threads that have taken on a higher priority). If a system does not allow preemptive multitasking, yielding control is the only way to get concurrency to happen.

When a thread is created, it takes its priority from the thread that created it. This way, threads run concurrently, with the scheduler switching back and forth between them. You can also explicitly set a thread's priority higher or lower, as long as it falls between the range `MIN_PRIORITY` and `MAX_PRIORITY`—values that the Thread class maintains. The default priority is set midway between these two values.

Advanced Synchronization

In addition to ensuring that only one chunk of code can be accessed at once, you can synchronize by splicing processes back together.

For example, here's pseudocode for the TownHall class's `main()` method:

```
create the MC
create the speakers
join the MC's thread with the thread that initiated it
close the town hall
```

What would happen if we did not attempt to join the MC's thread with the thread that initiated it (which is the thread that's running the `main()` method)? The town hall would close while the MC and the speakers were still inside hashing out the issues! In other words, we'd get output that looked something like this:

```
MC here: good morning.
speaker 4 stepping onto soapbox
speaker 1 stepping onto soapbox
speaker 3 stepping onto soapbox
speaker 0 stepping onto soapbox
speaker 0: music should be bought
speaker 2 stepping onto soapbox
Town Hall closing.
speaker 2: dogs should be made mandatory
speaker 2 stepping off soapbox
      .
      .
      .
```

To join a thread with the thread that initiated it, you simply call the thread's `join()` method. The MC for the town hall meeting does this as follows:

```
public static void main(String args[]) {

    // ... create the speakers ...

    MC georgeWill = new MC(podium);
    georgeWill.start();

    // ... let the speakers speak ...

    try {
       georgeWill.join();
    } catch (InterruptedException x) { }

    System.out.println("Town Hall closing.");
}
```

Since we're waiting for the MC thread to come to completion, we have to be prepared to handle an exception if it gets interrupted.

Implementing Runnable

Threads either can respond to process method calls directly—in particular, `run()`—or can transfer their control to a proxy. To do this, the proxy makes itself the thread's target and indicates it will implement the interface defined by Runnable:

```
class MyApplet extends Applet implements Runnable {

    // ... various applet methods

    public void myMethod() {
        Thread t = new Thread();
        t.target = this;
        t.start();
    }

    public void run() {
        System.out.println("the applet is handling run...");
    }
}
```

For example, let's look at the pendulum. So that the process that governs the pendulum's swing is running as a separate thread from anything else the application is doing, you can create a class called Pendulum that implements the Runnable interface. You can then create the thread, supplying an instance of your Pendulum class as the thread's target, as follows:

```
public class Pendulum implements Runnable {
    Thread myThread;

    public void startPendulum() {
        if (myThread == null) {
            myThread = new Thread(this, "Pendulum");
            myThread.start();
        }
}
```

When your thread goes to do its thing, it will look to your Pendulum class for its instructions. You can supply them like this:

```
/** Keep on swinging and redrawing the pendulum. */
public void run() {
    while (myThread != null) {
        swing();
        repaint();
    }
}
```

■   ERROR HANDLING

Error Reporting in C/C++

There are lots of ways to handle errors in C and C++. Three of them, covered in Part I, are as follows:

1. Return an error code.
2. Use `setjmp` and `longjmp`.
3. Use exceptions in C++.

In C++, especially, the issue is not so much that a good way doesn't exist but that there is no predefined standard. Even if you standardize on exceptions, what does this mean in C++? In C++, exceptions can be anything—your own objects, simple data types such as integers, objects that descend from an Exception class, and so on.

Exceptions in Java

Java standardizes error handling by defining an Exception class and a whole bunch of Exception subclasses. You can create your own Exception subclasses as well. (More precisely, in Java, you can throw any object that implements the Throwable interface, though, by convention, you should only throw instances of class Exception or instances of Exception's subclasses.)

By default, Java handles exceptions by printing an error message and then halting the thread. But you can catch the exceptions yourself and stop the default behavior from occurring. If you prefer, you can also rethrow the exception so that the default behavior still takes place.

You've seen a number of examples of exceptions in the sample code so far. The general relativity application defined a special Exception subclass called `WarpException`:

```
if (/* ... faster than light ... */)
   throw new WarpException();
```

This allowed us to signal that a particular type of error condition was found and let the caller handle the error in the way it finds most appropriate:

```
try {
    // ... calculate time dilation, etcetera ...
} catch (WarpException e) {
    System.out.println("Sorry, dilithium crystals have not
been discovered yet.");
}
```

When you throw an exception, you're outta there. You never return to the code that follows the `throw` statement. Note that you can throw a Throwable object whether an error actually occurred or not. All you have to do is set up an exception handler. But to say your code will quickly become unreadable is an understatement.

If you set up a bunch of `catch` statements to handle a particular exception, you can provide a kind of "catch all the rest of them" statement as the last one by looking for *any* exception (this is somewhat similar to (...) in C++):

```
try {
    // ... try something here ...
} catch (FirstException e) {
} catch (SecondException e) {
} catch (Exception e) {
}
```

The finally Block

Java provides a convenient mechanism to force a block of code to be executed even if an exception occurs. You define a finally statement as follows:

```
try {
    // do something
} finally {
    // clean up
}
```

Java interprets this the same way as

```
try {
    // do something
```

```
   } catch (Object e) {
      // clean up
      throw e;
   }
   // clean up
```

If you define a `finally` block, you're stuck with it. You'll execute the `finally` statement even if the code in the `try` block has a `continue` or a `break` in it—even if it has a `throw` or a `return`! How about that! Listing 11.5 shows an example of the amazing tenacity of `finally`.

Listing 11.5

```
class Tenacious {
   static public void main(String args[]) {
      try {
         myMethod1();
         myMethod2();
         myMethod3();
      } catch (Exception e) {
         System.out.println("Catching exception");
      }
   }

   static void myMethod1() {
      try {
         return;
      } finally {
         System.out.println("we tried to return...");
      }
   }

   static void myMethod2() {
top:
      try {
         break top;
       } finally {
         System.out.println("we tried to break...");
      }
   }

   static void myMethod3()
      throws Exception {
      try {
         throw(new Exception());
      } finally {
         System.out.println("we tried to throw an exception...");
      }
   }
}
```

Just as you'd expect, here's the output:

```
we tried to return...
we tried to break...
we tried to throw an exception...
Catching exception
```

When to Handle Exceptions

If a method might throw a particular exception, that method must declare this exception after its signature. We saw an example of this with `calcTimeDilation()`:

```
double calcTimeDilation(double distanceLightYr)
    throws WarpException {
        // ...
    }
```

If you use a method that might throw an exception, you should handle the exception yourself:

```
class EatInput {
   void myMethod () {
      try {
         while (System.in.read != -1);
      } catch (java.io.IOException e) {
         System.out.println("io error");
      }
   }
}
```

Or, you should indicate that an exception might percolate up the call stack from your method:

```
class EatInput {
   void myMethod () throws java.io.IOException {
      while (System.in.read != -1);
   }
}
```

Note that one way to "handle" an exception is to rethrow it:

```
class EatInput {
   void myMethod () throws java.io.IOException {
```

```
        try {
            while (System.in.read != -1);
        } catch (java.io.IOException e) {
            throw(e);
        }
    }
}
```

Java's Exceptions

All of Java's exceptions descend from class Exception. There are quite a number of possible exceptions. However, here are the ones you'll see and use most often.

ArithmeticException—You'll run into this exception if you try to do an illegal integer math operation, such as divide by 0. (Remember, floating-point values don't throw exceptions.)

ArrayIndexOutOfBoundsException—If you try to access an element beyond the bounds of an array, Java will throw this exception.

ClassCastException—If you cast an object to a type that is not in its branch of the class tree, Java will throw this exception. (For example, you'll see this if you try to cast an Integer object to a String.)

InterruptedException—If a thread interrupts a thread unexpectedly, you can receive this exception.

IOException—This indicates an I/O exception occurred, such as reading past the end of a file.

NullPointerException—If you use a null pointer illegally, you'll see this exception. One common way to make this exception appear is if you set up back-to-back method calls and the first method returns a null value rather than an object, as in firstMethod().secondMethod().

OutOfMemoryException—You'll see this exception if you run out of working memory.

There are many other exceptions that Java defines. Check out the package APIs for even more.

■ SUMMARY

This chapter showed you how Java expands on some features that are part of C++ and how Java implements multitasking. Arrays and strings are implemented as first-class objects. They are not merely blocks of memory whose bits and bytes you manipulate directly; instead, they have well-defined interfaces and protect their data.

Java makes it easy to coordinate among asynchronous threads. When multitasking occurs, the order of events is inherently unpredictable. This could lead to all sorts of problems, but Java makes synchronizing among these various (essentially random) events part of the language, which makes the programmer's task a breeze.

Java assists with error handling. While exceptions exist in C++, Java formalizes their use by requiring methods to declare which exceptions they throw. Java also provides a number of standard exceptions that you can use and expand on in your own applications.

■ WHAT'S NEXT?

Before we move on to the class libraries, the next chapter makes explicit any remaining questions you might have between C++ and Java. While C and C++ are immediate predecessors of Java, Java is not a superset of these languages. Certain features that were in C++ have been removed entirely from Java. And, while you cannot control registers, demand in-line expansion, or order allocated memory to be freed immediately, you can participate in these events and hint to Java when these events should occur and what should happen when they do.

12

Covering the Rest of It

Did we cover everything? Well, almost. Chapter 12 mops up by poking into all the remaining C and C++ hiding places. In addition, while you can't always demand that memory management work a certain way, you can hint to Java how your code is expected to work so that it can perform optimizations when it can. In this chapter, you'll learn what you can't do, what you can do instead, and how to optimize your code.

■ WHAT YOU CAN'T DO

Let's start off by touching on some items ignored so far. Mostly, these are things that you cannot do in Java. Some of these features might cause you to rethink your implementation as compared with C++.

Unions

While you can cast data types, you can't overlay the same piece of memory with two different variables defined as different data types.

References

Using references in C++, you can define two variables that refer to the same address. References are handy, for example, for changing an object in the return value of a function call. They are also useful if you are passing a very large structure to another function and want to pass the structure by reference without using pointers.

References are basically handles to objects in Java, and objects are always passed by reference. The other capabilities provided by references are not supported in Java.

Preprocessing

There is no preprocessor in Java—at least, not one that you can control directly. Again, where C/C++ comes down on the side of programmer control, Java takes the tack of ease of programming and ease of understanding. Without a preprocessor, there is no need to search through header files or unravel various # directives to see how your code will be expanded before compilation.

Macros

If there's no preprocessor, there surely aren't macros. This kills off a slew of common mistakes, such the classic problems of macros expanding into lines of code you didn't intend.

Though there aren't macros, this does not mean that you can't have code that's expanded inline. Instead, Java finds a cleaner way to indicate this. (See the section on inline functions that is given later in this chapter.)

Conditional Compilation

Without preprocessor variables, every piece of code you write gets compiled. You cannot use `#ifdefs`, for example, to include or exclude code according to preprocessor variables during compilation.

Templates

Templates are necessary in C++ because there is no actual root class. In C++, if you need to define a container class and you want the same basic behavior for a variety of different objects, you can define your container class once, generically, and then tell the preprocessor to implement the template for particular objects.

In Java, there is no need to do this. Your container classes can be defined once to work with the root class, class Object. In this way, your container classes will work for any object in the system, and there is no need to ever define a template.

Header Files

Now, you might be so used to header files that discovering you can't use them might come as a shock. But think about what you normally put in header files—constants, macros, structures, function prototypes, and so on. You don't have these things in Java, so you don't need header files!

But wait! What about including additional data and behavior outside the code you write? What if you want to access a third-party class library or one of your own?

You already know how to do this: You can import classes you need from other packages. Since Java is a dynamic language, with the interpreter linking in the class files as required, there is no need to define your classes in static header files.

Variable-Length Parameter Lists

One last thing here: You can't define variable-length parameter lists the way you can in C++. Along with this, you cannot assign default values for variables within the parameter list.

■ SUBSTITUTIONS

Structures and Typedefs

Instead of structures, just use objects. The only new types you're allowed to define are classes (including arrays) and interfaces. If you want something as close to an old-style C structure as you can get, create a public class that only contains public instance variables.

Functions

What if you want to do something that doesn't require a particular instance or seem to belong with any particular class? Like some little utility that you pass a value to and it does something, such as return a result. You know, like a *function*. One thing you could do is create a special class to maintain all the utility code you need to write and make these methods static. For example, if you need a couple of functions that read from the standard input and write to the standard output, you could create your own utility class to contain them:

```
public class MyUtilities {
    public void writeToScreen(String s) {
        System.out.println(s);
    }

    public String readFromKeyboard() {
        ...
    }
}
```

Well now, this is a little like having a function, isn't it? To execute this behavior, you simply say

```
MyUtilities.writeToScreen("Hello, World");
```

and

```
input = MyUtilities.readFromKeyboard();
```

Call by Reference

One use for pointers and addresses is passing a value to a function by reference. This lets the function you call update the argument value directly because the function can directly access the argument's address.

In Java, you always pass arguments by reference, except for simple data types (`int`, `double`, and so on), which are passed by value. That is, you can change the fields of an object that you pass, and you are really changing the original object, not a local copy of it.

If you want to pass a simple data type by reference, how can you do it? One quick way is to create an array. You can even create an array of one element if you wish. Put the simple data type you want to "pass by reference" into the array. Now, you can pass the array to your method, and you have, in effect, passed a variable containing an atomic value by reference!

For example, suppose you have an `int` that you'd like to pass by reference. Listing 12.1 shows how you can do it.

Listing 12.1

```
public class Caller {
    public static void main(String[] args) {
        int[] myArray = new int[1];
        myArray[0] = 50;

        System.out.println(myArray[0]);
        doubleValue(myArray);
        System.out.println(myArray[0]);
    }

    static void doubleValue(int[] myArray) {
        myArray[0] *= 2;
    }
}
```

The output for this little program is

```
50
100
```

As you can see, we modified the `int` value `myArray[0]` directly. That is, in C/C++, you can write code as follows:

```
void doubleValue(int *referenceVariable) {
    *referenceVariable *= 2;
}

main() {
    int referenceVariable = 2;
    println("%ld", referenceVariable);
    doubleValue(&referenceVariable);
    println("%ld", referenceVariable);
}
```

This code does essentially the same thing as we did in Listing 12.1.

Constants and Preprocessor Variables

You already know you can create constants accessible to any object throughout your application. For example, you could declare a constant for the point value for chess pieces as follows:

```
public static final QUEEN_POINTS = 9;
public static final ROOK_POINTS = 5;
public static final BISHOP_POINTS = 3;
public static final KNIGHT_POINTS = 3;
public static final PAWN_POINTS = 1;
```

You would, of course, put these definitions into some class, such as one called `ChessPiece`. However, you can create something much more akin to how you think of constants by putting them into their own class. For example, you could create a class called `MyConstants` that only defines constants. When you wanted to access a constant, you would know right where to find it:

```
MyConstants.ROOK_POINTS
```

Multiple Inheritance

Although you can't implement multiple inheritance in Java, you can share characteristics by defining interfaces. (Recall that Chapter 9 discussed interfaces in detail.)

■ OPTIMIZATIONS

Freeing Memory

In C/C++, when you allocate memory, you can also free it explicitly. In C, if you ask for a chunk of memory as in

```
*buffer = malloc(1024);
```

you must remember to return this memory to the heap when you're done:

```
free(buffer);
```

In C++, you can pair up `new` with `delete` to allocate and then return memory to the heap. You can also create destructor methods that can perform last-minute closing of files, freeing of buffers, and so on. But when Java runs the show, how do you get into the act and assist with cleaning up memory? There is a way.

Java doesn't have destructors that are always called and that follow the standard C++ syntax, such as

```
object::~object() {
};
```

However, you *can* have your object help out with cleaning up system resources when the garbage collector comes along and squooshes it. If you define a `finalize()` method for your object, then you've enabled finalization for your object. At some time after the system has determined that your object is a candidate for garbage collection, this finalize method *might* get called.

The word "might" is definitely a little vague here. The problem with being more exact is that finalization occurs as part of garbage collection, which is happening asynchronously in the background as a low-priority process.

If you try to help out your object and call `finalize()` directly, which is perfectly legal, you have no guarantee that Java won't call it again when it really does go away. So if you do call it directly, you have to keep track of what you've done so that you don't perform the same cleanup twice (that is, if doing so is harmful).

Finalization is good for when you want to optimize the way your program works, perhaps by cleaning up references to files that you no longer need when your object goes away. Finalization is pretty cool because, by definition, if the system is calling `finalize()`, you have no way to get to your object. That's why it's a candidate for garbage collection in the first place. Yet, you can still plant some code in your object that runs even though you can no longer access it. In other words, since you're not in control of exactly when your object goes away, this is your back door into Java's garbage collection. (You can, however, invoke the garbage collector via the System or Runtime class.)

There are some situations when you can virtually guarantee your `finalize()` method will or will not be called. For example, as you'll see shortly, I had to rig the sample program in Listing 12.2 so that it stuck around long enough for the garbage collector to run even after I invoked it directly and to see that I didn't have a reference to my object anymore. (This little sample is also great proof that garbage collection is actually occurring!)

If the program ended too soon, my object would never get finalized. Finalization is not identical to a destructor. Your `finalize()` doesn't necessarily get called, even when your program ends and your object goes out of scope.

You can also force finalization to happen if you

- call it yourself
- force garbage collection to occur (assuming the object in question really is a candidate for garbage collection) by using the static method `System.gc()`
- execute `System.runFinalization()`, which runs the `finalize()` method on all objects awaiting garbage collection (without necessarily performing garbage collection)

Listing 12.2 is an example in which Java calls a `finalize()` method when it has detected that the object is a candidate for garbage collection.

Listing 12.2

```
class FinalizeExample {
    public static void main(String args[]) {
        Test1 a = new Test1();
        Test2 b = new Test2();

        a.start();
        b.start();

        a = null;
        System.gc();
    }
}

class Test1 {
    void finalize() {
        System.out.println("We're in finalize");
    }
}
```

```
class Test2 extends Thread {
   public void run() {
      for (int i = 0; i < 2; i++) {
         System.out.println("waiting...." + i);
         try {
         sleep(2000); // 2 seconds
         } catch (java.lang.InterruptedException e) {
            System.out.println("interrupted exception");
         }
      }
   }
}
```

The output from this program is

```
waiting....0
We're in finalize
waiting....1
```

In other words, we created an object but then killed off our reference to it. However, the program did not end right away. Instead, a thread hung around counting off time. The garbage collector was able to grab some time to run, found there was an object we couldn't access anymore, and zapped it. When it did, Java called its `finalize()` method, and so we were able to print out a string indicating it was leaving.

Note that you don't have to call your inherited `finalize()` method. The system will do this for you.

Inline Functions

For performance reasons, you can ask the C++ compiler to eliminate some of the overhead involved with calling a function. Rather than pushing arguments onto a stack, storing registers, and so on, you can request that a particular function be expanded and used inline.

While you cannot issue these exact directives in Java, you can hint to Java that it can expand a particular method in place if it wishes. (It's only a hint because whether it does so or not is up to the particular implementation of Java and is at least partially based on whether the method in question is "small" enough.)

How do you give this hint? You use your old friend, the keyword `final`. If a method is final, Java knows it won't be overridden, making it safe to expand inline.

Suppressing Optimization With volatile

While this section concerns itself with optimizations, there is another keyword you can use to tell the compiler not to make optimizations for a particular variable. To tell the compiler that a variable might be changed by another thread, you can use the keyword `volatile`, just as you would in C/C++. Before we look into this, keep in mind that this keyword is really much more important in C/C++ than it is in Java. In Java, you will almost always use the synchronized keyword instead to achieve the results you're after.

Here's an example. Say you have two instance variables set up like this:

```
int x = 2;
int[1000000] arr;
```

and your program calls a method that loops through all of the million items in the array, changing the value of each item in the array as follows:

```
void myMethod() {
    for (int i = 0; i < 999999; i++)
        arr[i] += x * x;
}
```

This code squares the value of x and then adds it to the array element. The tricky part comes into play because compilers are smart, and Java compilers are no exception. The compiler will look at this loop and think, "Hmm... I see that in this block of code, I can treat the value x * x like a constant. So, rather than performing a million multiplications, I can create a temporary variable outside of the loop and do the multiplication once." Here's how the compiler might change the code if you could see it:

```
void myMethod() {
    int xsquared = x * x; // temporary variable
```

```
        for (int i = 0; i < 999999; i++)
            arr[i] += xsquared;
    }
```

This is all fine so far. The problem is that Java is multithreaded. If another thread comes along, interrupts `myMethod()`, and changes the instance variable x, then xsquared will no longer reflect the current value of x for the rest of the loop.

Whether the optimization just outlined is correct or not is a question of the intent for your program. If you wanted to add the *same* x squared value to *all* array items, you don't want the value of x to change right in the middle of the loop. A good way to do this in Java is to write an access method for the x instance variable, and declare both `myMethod()` and the access method to be synchronized. Now only one thread can get at this value at any one time.

If you do want to suppress the optimization without synchronizing the methods, you can use the volatile keyword, like this:

```
        volatile int x = 2;
```

Now, the effect of `myMethod()` will be to square the current value of x before adding it to the array, even if x changes right in the middle of the loop.

■ KEYWORDS

A Summary of What's in Java

To be complete, this section covers the keywords in Java, which should now be fairly familiar to you. After this listing, the C and C++ keywords that you cannot use in Java will be quickly reviewed.

Organizing Classes
- `package` specifies the class in a particular source file should belong to the named package.
- `import` requests the named class or classes be imported into the current application.

Defining Classes

- `interface` defines global data and method signatures that can be shared among classes.
- `class` defines a collection of related data and behavior.
- `extends` indicates which class to subclass.
- `implements` indicates the interface for which a new class will supply methods.

Keywords for Classes and Variables

- `abstract` specifies the class cannot be instantiated directly.
- `public` means the class, method, or variable can be accessed from anywhere.
- `private` means only the class defining the method or variable can access it.
- `protected` means only the defining class and its subclasses can access the method or variable.
- `static` specifies a class method or variable.
- `synchronized` indicates only one object or class can access this variable or method at a time.
- `volatile` tells the compiler this variable may change asynchronously due to threads.
- `final` means this variable or method cannot be changed by subclasses.
- `native` links a method to native code.

Simple Data Types

- `long` is a 64-bit integer value.
- `int` is a 32-bit integer value.
- `short` is a 16-bit integer value.
- `byte` is an 8-bit integer value.
- `double` is a 64-bit floating-point value.
- `float` is a 32-bit floating-point value.
- `char` is a 16-bit Unicode character.
- `boolean` is a true or false value.
- `void` indicates a method does not return a value.

Values and Variables

- `false` is a Boolean value.
- `true` is a Boolean value.

- `this` refers to the current instance in an instance method.
- `super` refers to the immediate superclass in an instance method.
- `null` represents a nonexistent instance.

Exception Handling

- `throw` throws an exception.
- `try` marks the stack so that if an exception is thrown, it will unwind to this point.
- `catch` catches an exception.
- `finally` says execute this block of code regardless of exception error handling flow.

Instance Creation and Testing

- `new` creates new instances.
- `instanceof` tests whether an instance derives from a particular class or interface.

Control Flow

- `switch` tests a variable.
- `case` executes a particular block of code according to the value tested in the switch.
- `default` means the default block of code executes if no matching `case` statement was found.
- `break` breaks out of a particular block of code.
- `continue` continues with the next iteration of a loop.
- `return` returns from a method, optionally passing back a value.
- `do` performs some statement or set of statements.
- `if` tests for a condition and performs some action if true.
- `else` performs some action if the above test was false.
- `for` signifies iteration.
- `while` performs some action while a condition is true.

Not Used Yet, But Reserved

- `byvalue`
- `const`
- `goto`
- `cast`
- `future`
- `generic`

- `inner`
- `operator`
- `outer`
- `rest`
- `var`

Keywords Not Available from C

So where does this leave us? There are a number of C-specific keywords that are not a part of Java:

```
asm, auto, enum, extern, register, signed, sizeof, struct,
typedef, union, unsigned, wchar_t
```

Keywords Not Available from C++

And what about C++? Here are the keywords in C++ that do not appear in Java:

```
bool, const_cast, delete, dynamic_cast, friend, inline, mutable,
namespace, reinterpret_cast, static_cast, template, typeid, using,
virtual
```

■ SUMMARY

This chapter provided a look at the remaining items between C++ and Java that this book had not yet covered. Java always strives for ease of programming correct code. Sometimes, this means that the default behavior is not the fastest. However, the default behavior will always allow your programs to run correctly, which is not necessarily the case in C/C++.

Some features of C++, such as templates and macros, are implemented more cleanly in Java. Some optimizations, such as whether or not variables can be placed in registers or methods can be expanded inline, are not directly under programmer control in Java, as they are in C++. Instead, sometimes you can only hint to the Java compiler and runtime environment how you would like your code executed.

For those items that were not implemented in Java, you'll probably notice a theme: They are ways programmers get in trouble in C and C++. As always, Java comes down on the side of encouraging programmers to write good, clean code.

■ WHAT'S NEXT?

Now that all the basics of the Java language have been covered, we're ready to explore Java's class libraries. All sorts of powerful features are available in Java's packages that allow you to jumpstart your application development. In particular, the next chapter reviews a number of fun and interesting programs and examines how Java's packages helped in their creation.

13

Working with Java's Packages

Like C and C++, Java provides many extensions to the language that make the programmer's task much simpler. These extensions are provided through separate packages. In addition to the same types of utilities you'd find in the C and C++ libraries, Java's packages also include support for graphical, multithreaded, Internet programming. Java's platform-independent APIs help programmers build advanced applications quickly and easily. While a complete tour of Java's packages is not within the scope of this book, Chapter 13 does provide an in-depth look at how to use Java's packages by examining sample programs that illustrate their capabilities.

■ JAVA'S PACKAGES AND THE EXAMPLE APPLICATIONS

Five Useful Packages

The packages covered here include `lang`, `net`, `awt`, `io`, and `util`. (The applet package is covered in Chapter 14.)

203

java.lang

`java.lang` includes classes for the basic objects in the system, including the ability to use the standard input and output. You've already used the System class to perform command line input and output. You've also used the Object class and the wrapper classes (Integer, Float, and so on) throughout this book. This chapter will show you some additional methods defined in the classes in this package.

java.net

`java.net` defines classes for communicating over the Internet. This includes protocols that can speak TCP/IP (Transfer Control Protocol/Internet Protocol), http (Hypertext Transport Protocol), and HTML (Hypertext Markup Language). This package also contains classes that allow your Java application to understand Internet resources such as URLs (Universal Resource Locators). This chapter will look at some of the ways you can use the classes in this package to include Internet communication in your own applications.

java.awt

`java.awt` is an acronym for Abstract Windows Toolkit. This package consists of classes you can use to construct graphical user interfaces (GUIs). You can also perform graphics operations in a way that's independent of any particular windowing API. This package includes many GUI elements, ranging from buttons to text fields to windows. You've already seen Frames, Panels, TextFields, Labels, and Buttons. This chapter will survey some additional UI components and will delve into LayoutManagers and how you handle events.

java.io

`java.io` includes definitions for streams and files. This chapter will consider classes that allow you to interact with your operating system's native file system. You'll see how to obtain handles to directories and files and how to read the contents of files.

java.util

`java.util` implements dates, random numbers, stacks, hash tables, and other useful utility classes. This chapter will cover all of these.

Six Educational Applications

We'll use six, fun Java applications to explore these packages. Some of these applications appeared earlier in this book. This section provides a short overview to how these applications work. After this overview, we'll turn to Java's packages and see how these applications take advantage of the functionality these packages have to offer. Remember, the full listings for these applications are presented in Appendix B. This chapter aims to highlight how these applications take advantage of Java's packages and classes to provide powerful features with a minimum of code.

JavaWalker

JavaWalker uses the `lang`, `awt`, `util`, and `net` packages to walk the links from one Web page to the next. Figure 13.1 shows what the user sees when running JavaWalker. Note that new links are added in real-time as JavaWalker weaves its way through the Web.

JavaWalker presents four buttons, a text field, and a list. Users enter a URL into the text field and then use the buttons to tell JavaWalker to

Figure 13.1   JavaWalker in action

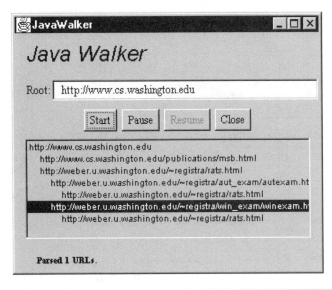

start or stop walking through the Web. When JavaWalker walks through the Web, it takes the following steps:

1. Accesses the Web page given by the root URL.
2. Parses the page, looking for other Web addresses.
3. Presents these Web addresses in a list.
4. Picks the first Web address in the list that has not yet been investigated.
5. Accesses this page.
6. Returns to step 2 to parse, and so on.

JavaWalker creates a thread to access the Web. Creating a separate thread for walking the Web allows users to continue interacting with the application, even while the application is performing time-intensive operations such as opening http connections, reading files over the network, parsing files, and so on. When the user clicks the start or resume button, the thread starts. When the user clicks the pause button, the thread stops. The close button ends the application.

JavaWalker illustrates a number of classes from Java's packages:

From java.net
- URLs interact with the Internet at a very high level, bypassing the details of packets, socket I/O, and so on.

From java.awt
- LayoutManagers organize the user interface.
- Lists present text in a window.

From java.lang
- Threads perform background processing and access to the Web.
- Strings parse the data coming in over the Web.

From java.util
- Hashtables remember which pages have already been visited.
- Vectors keep track of what to parse next.

JavaTalker

JavaTalker uses the `io` and `net` packages to establish a connection between two computers connected to the Internet. One person launches

JavaTalker as a server; the other starts up JavaTalker as a client and connects to the server application.

Once the connection is established, both invocations of the application start two threads. These threads handle the following:

1. They receive data from the socket and write it using the standard output.
2. They receive data from the standard input and write it to the socket.

Figure 13.2 shows a JavaTalker session in progress. When one person types a message and hits enter, the other person sees the data appear on the monitor.

JavaTalker uses classes that illustrate some lower-level Internet communication and input/output:

From java.net
- InetAddress maintains the host name for the server used to establish the Internet connection.
- ServerSocket provides the socket for the server.
- Socket provides the socket for the client.

Figure 13.2   A JavaTalker session

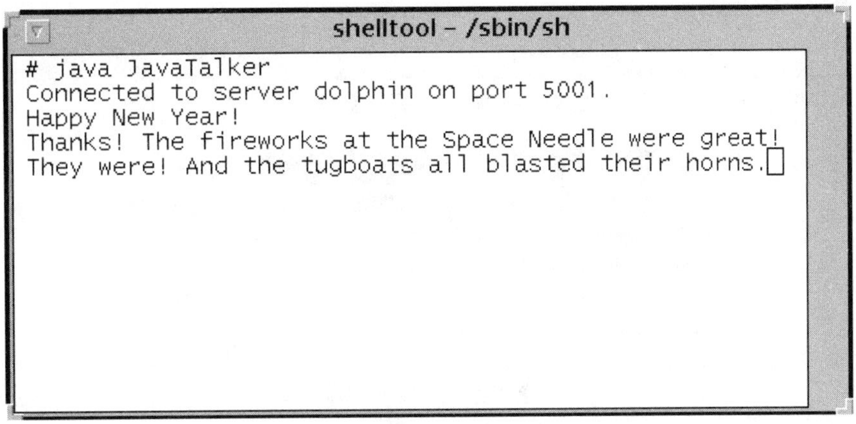

```
shelltool – /sbin/sh
# java JavaTalker
Connected to server dolphin on port 5001.
Happy New Year!
Thanks! The fireworks at the Space Needle were great!
They were! And the tugboats all blasted their horns.
```

From java.io

- DataInputStream is used to read data from the standard input and the socket.
- DataOutputStream is used to write data to the standard output and the socket.

FileBrowser

FileBrowser uses the `lang`, `awt`, and `io` packages to present a list of files for the user to browse through. Figure 13.3 shows what FileBrowser looks like as the user interacts with it.

The FileBrowser application presents a list of Java source files that exist in the directory from which the user invoked FileBrowser. As shown by Figure 13.4, when the user selects a file in the list and clicks the view button, FileBrowser presents the selected file in a separate window.

Note that FileBrowser is ripe for adding new features. Two great features would be the following:

1. An additional file choice of ".." would allow the user to go up one directory node.
2. A choice for selecting the filter to apply to the list of files in the directory being viewed would allow the user to access files other than those ending in ".java".

In the interest of keeping this application simple, these features are left unimplemented.

Figure 13.3 FileBrowser application presenting a list of files

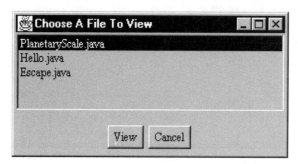

Figure 13.4   FileBrowser application displaying the contents of a selected file

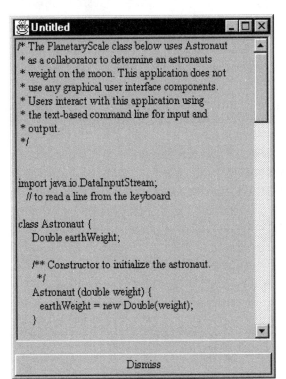

FileBrowser uses the following packages and classes:

From java.lang
- Strings parse the files in the current directory.

From java.io
- Files get a handle to a directory node.
- FileInputStreams get a handle to a file.
- DataInputStreams read the contents for a file.

From java.awt
- Frames create a separate window hierarchy in which to view the selected file.
- Lists present the list of files and the contents of the selected file.

Pendulum

Pendulum uses the `lang` and `awt` packages to simulate a pendulum. While we've touched on some aspects of this application, this chapter presents some new details. Pendulum uses some classes and methods not yet covered in this book:

From java.lang

■ The Math class performs mathematical operations such as trigonometry.

From java.awt

■ Components respond to events, such as mouse movements.
■ Graphics perform draw operations, such as drawing circles and lines.

TownHall

TownHall uses the `lang` and `util` packages to model a meeting. As described in Chapter 11, the TownHall application primarily illustrates multithreading. Here is another package and class used by TownHall:

From java.lang

■ Random generates random numbers.

PlanetaryScale

PlanetaryScale calculates an astronaut's moon weight. This application was explained in Chapter 7. This chapter uses the application to illustrate a particular aspect of the AWT:

From java.awt

■ LayoutManagers affect the positioning of the UI components.

This chapter also points out some particularly useful methods in the libraries when these applications don't already do so.

■ SOME MORE JAVA.LANG EXAMPLES

The package `java.lang` defines the basic system classes: Object, Math, System, Integer, and so on. Since every Java application must at least use the Object class, this package is automatically included in your Java applications without the need to explicitly import it.

This book has already explored a variety of classes from `java.lang`. This section goes into more detail involving the String and Math classes to illustrate some additional behavior you might find useful in your own applications.

Advanced String Examples

The String class is loaded with functionality! The URLParser class in JavaWalker, for example, makes use of a number of String methods to parse the Web pages it accesses:

1. `toLowerCase()` converts the text to all lowercase characters.
2. `indexOf()` finds the first occurrence of another string.
3. `substring()` returns a string representing a piece of the original string.
4. `charAt()` retrieves a particular character from a string.
5. `Character.isSpace()` tests whether a particular character is a space.
6. `startsWith()` tests whether a string starts with a particular substring.

URLParser looks through the raw HTML document it retrieves over the Web and finds Web pages of the form

```
http://xxx/.../xxx.html
```

For the purposes of keeping the example here relatively straightforward, URLParser only identifies links that begin with "http:" and end with ".html".

```
class URLParser {
    String contents;

    public URLParser (String data) {
        contents = data;
    }
```

```java
public Queue parse () {
    int tag, quote, http, html, last;
    Queue q = new Queue ();
    String href;
    String text = new String (contents);
    text = text.toLowerCase ();

    try {
        last = 0;
        while (last < contents.length ()) {
        if ((tag = text.indexOf ("<a", last)) < 0)
            break;
        last = tag + 2;
        while (Character.isSpace (text.charAt (last))) last++;
        if (text.startsWith ("href", last)) {
            quote = text.indexOf ("\"", last);
            http = text.indexOf ("\"http:", last);
            if ((http < 0) || (http != quote))
                continue;
            quote = text.indexOf ("\"", http + 6);
              html = text.indexOf (".html\"", http + 6);
            if ((html < 0) || (html + 5 != quote)) {
                last = http + 6;
                continue;
            }
            href = contents.substring (http + 1, html + 5);
            q.enqueue (new URL (href));
            last = html + 6;
        }
        }
    } catch (StringIndexOutOfBoundsException e) {
      System.out.println (e.getMessage () + ": Parse error.");
    } catch (MalformedURLException e) {
        System.out.println (e.getMessage () + ": Bad URL.");
    }
    return q;
    }
}
```

For another example of using some advanced String methods, check out FileBrowser. FileBrowser obtains the current directory's list of files (see the section later in this chapter on files and the `java.io` package for more information). Each file is obtained as a string containing the file name. FileBrowser adds each String instance to a String array called `file_list`. Then, FileBrowser looks through this array of Strings and identifies those files that end in a particular suffix—in this case, with the suffix defined previously to identify Java source code. FileBrowser uses the very convenient String method `endsWith()` to identify those strings ending with the ".java" identifier:

```
String filter_suffix = new String(".java");
String[] file_list;

// ... place Strings representing files into file_list ...

for (int i = 0; i < file_list.length; i++) {
        if (file_list[i].endsWith(filter_suffix)) {
            // .. display this file in the list ...
        }
}
```

Math Examples

Like the standard C `math.h` library, the Math class provides a number of useful methods for performing math calculations. The Math class also tosses in methods such as `abs()` and `max()`. All are implemented as static methods so that you don't have to instantiate the Math class to use them.

The Pendulum application uses the Math class fairly extensively. For example, here's how to find the next position in the pendulum's arc:

1. Calculate an increment to move the pendulum (note that we use the constant `Math.PI`):

```
theta = p.cord.angle + (speed * (Math.PI/divisions) *
        (double)dir);
```

2. Determine where the weight at the end of the pendulum should be drawn using the Math class's trig methods:

```
xpos = (int)(Math.sin(theta) * (double)p.cord.length) +
        Cord.CORD_PIVOT_X;
ypos = (int)(Math.cos(theta) * (double)p.cord.length) +
        Cord.CORD_PIVOT_Y;
```

The Pendulum application also uses Math class methods when calculating the speed at which to swing the pendulum. Given the length of the pendulum, we can calculate the speed at which it's traveling when it reaches the bottom of its swing. The square of the speed will be 2 times gravity times pendulum length times (1 – cosine (initial angle)):

```
double fastestSpeed = Math.sqrt(2.0 * 9.81 *
        (double)p.cord.length *
            (1.0 - Math.cos(p.cord.angle)) );
```

Other Language Classes

Some other useful classes in the `java.lang` package are as follows:

- ThreadGroup organizes threads into collections of similar threads.
- Runtime implements runtime-specific functionality, such as executing calls to the system library or exiting the system.

Threads can only access other threads within the same ThreadGroup. ThreadGroups allow you to start and stop threads en masse. They allow you to enumerate over the threads in the group, check on the max priority of the threads in the group, and perform other useful tasks. You can also create hierarchies of ThreadGroups if you'd like to by including ThreadGroups inside other ThreadGroups. (If you do create hierarchies, note that threads cannot access other threads in their parent group.)

■ GRAPHICS WITH JAVA.AWT

The package `java.awt` defines all of the classes required for constructing a graphical user interface. In Chapter 7, you got your feet wet with the Abstract Windows Toolkit; now, you'll wade in a little deeper.

Positioning, Fonts, and Pixels

There are situations when graphics operations in Java are platform independent, and you should definitely strive to take advantage of these situations. For example, you can use a layout manager, as described shortly, to position the components of your user interface in a way that's independent of the pixel sizes and dots per inch of the monitor on which a particular user is running your application.

One way around platform dependence is to position the elements of your user interface based on fonts. Java's classes sometimes take this into account for you. For example, if you indicate you'd like a button to use a particular font, the default button behavior is for it to expand so that its name still fits in its boundaries when displayed with the font you've indicated.

You can specify a font by naming the font, specifying its style, and defining its size in the Font object's constructor. You can then use the Component method `setFont()` to attach this font to the UI element you'd like to use this font:

```
Button b = new Button("click me");
b.setFont (new Font ("Helvetica", Font.ITALIC, 60));
```

However, for many of Java's low-level graphics operations—such as drawing lines or indicating exact positions on the screen—Java uses pixels to measure distances. This means that you should be wary of specifying locations that might make your user interface look different on high-resolution versus low-resolution monitors. For example, while a value of 110 pixels might be one inch on your monitor, it might be only half an inch on someone else's.

Again, using fonts helps you get around this problem. For example, you might want to center a String in a window. You can do this by getting the information concerning the current font for your Graphics object and then measuring the width and height of the String you'd like to draw:

```
// ... g is the Graphics object for your component ...
// ... s is the String to draw ...
FontMetrics fm = g.getFontMetrics();
int width = fm.stringWidth(s);
int height = fm.stringHeight();
```

Armed with the dimensions of the String, you can now position this String within another component by finding your component's dimension and then offsetting for the size of the String.

Java's Layout Managers

Layout managers allow you to specify the look of your user interface in a general way. For example, you can request that a label appear at the top of a window and a button appear in the center. Even if the user resizes your window, the layout manager will still follow your instructions. For example, it will move the label higher up, if necessary, and will place the button into the new center. Layout managers make sure your components still look good and are arranged how you want them, no matter what the monitor resolution or window sizes.

A default layout manager is automatically created and assigned to your containers as you create them. If you wish, you can override the default layout manager in one of three ways:

1. Set the container's layout manager to `null` and use absolute values to specify the components' positions within your container. (Not recommended if you can help it!)
2. Instantiate one of five Java classes that implements the LayoutManager interface and set the container's layout manager to this instance. (Definitely!)
3. Create your own class that implements the LayoutManager interface; instantiate this and set the container's layout manager to this instance. (Only for the brave!)

Java defines five classes that implement the LayoutManager interface: BorderLayout, FlowLayout, CardLayout, GridLayout, and the mighty GridBagLayout. BorderLayout is the default layout for Windows (Dialogs and Frames). FlowLayout is the default layout for Panels.

We'll use our little PlanetaryScale application to show how different layout managers affect the positioning of UI components. There are only two components in PlanetaryScale: a text field and a label. You'll see what happens to these in turn with each of the layout managers.

FlowLayout

FlowLayout adds items to containers left to right, centering each component within its row. The FlowLayout will add more rows if it runs out of room to place additional components. FlowLayouts are intended to be used with buttons (as in a menu bar). FlowLayouts define three

Figure 13.5   FlowLayout with two components in the same row

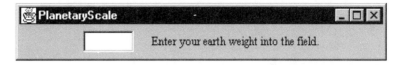

constants to set the alignment. These values are LEFT, CENTER, and RIGHT.

FlowLayouts are the default for Panels, and PlanetaryScale uses a Panel. The effect of a FlowLayout is that the UI elements can jump around depending on how the user has sized the panel. For example, when the application is wide enough to fit the button and the text field on the same row, the components are arranged as in Figure 13.5.

However, if the user resizes the panel so that it is no longer wide enough to contain both components, the FlowLayout will put the label in its own row, below the text field, as Figure 13.6 shows.

Figure 13.6   FlowLayout with two components on different rows

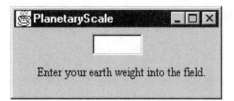

One consequence of using a FlowLayout is that you cannot provide instructions in your labels, such as "Enter your weight into the text field on the left", since that's not necessarily where the FlowLayout will put it!

BorderLayout

BorderLayout places components in one of five locations: north, south, east, west, and center. (All extra space is placed in the center.) Unlike using a FlowLayout, using a BorderLayout will keep the components where we put them.

For example, suppose we set the layout manager for the panel to be a BorderLayout and position the text field at the top and the label at the bottom, like this:

```
setLayout(new BorderLayout());
resize(400,200);

textField = new TextField(6);
add("North", textField);

label = new Label("Enter your earth weight into the field.");
add("South", label);
```

Figure 13.7shows what will happen when we compile and run. As you can see, the text field stretches to fill the top of the panel. (The label also stretches to fill up the bottom of the panel.) Even if the user resizes the panel, the text field will continue to occupy the top and stretch from the left side to the right.

Figure 13.7 BorderLayout with components at the top and bottom

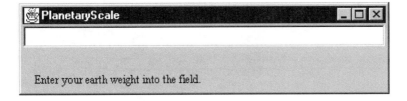

If we assign the text field to be "East" and the label to be "West", we get the result shown in Figure 13.8. The components will continue to occupy these regions of the panel no matter how the user resizes it.

GridLayout

GridLayout places components in a grid consisting of equally sized elements. You specify the number of rows and columns for the Grid-Layout when you create it. GridLayouts add components to the container by filling in each column in the first row before moving to the second row, then filling in the second row before moving to the third, and so on.

Figure 13.8   BorderLayout with components on the left and right

For example, suppose we define a GridLayout with 1 row and 2 columns and assign it to the panel, like this:

```
setLayout(new GridLayout(1,2));
```

The GridLayout will arrange the text field and label as in Figure 13.9. Notice the regions of the grid are equally sized and the elements fill up those regions.

Figure 13.9   GridLayout that is 1 row and 2 columns

If we arrange the grid as 2 rows and 1 column, we get the display in Figure 13.10. As before, if the user resizes the panel, the grid cells also resize to remain equal, and the components inside the cells expand or shrink to remain within their cells.

Figure 13.10   GridLayout that is 2 rows and 1 column

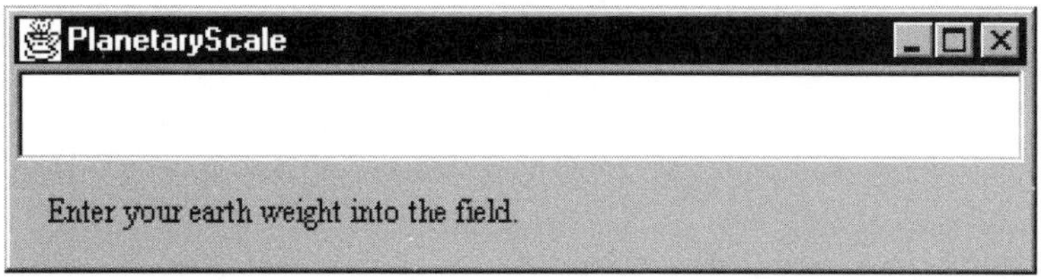

CardLayout

CardLayout is used to present different options depending on a choice the user has made. The intent of a CardLayout is to allow you to maintain a set of cards, so to speak, that you can flip through and present one at a time. CardLayouts define methods to allow you to flip to the first, next, or last card. You can also go directly to a card if you've named it.

For example, suppose we want to flip between two cards that maintain information for equations of the rich and famous. Figure 13.11 shows what the FamousEquations Frame subclass looks like when it's first launched.

Figure 13.11 CardLayout showing the first card

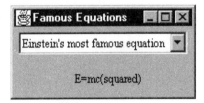

Figure 13.12 shows what the CardLayout displays after the user interacts with the choice list to select another choice.

Figure 13.12 CardLayout showing the second card

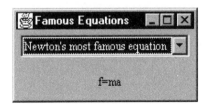

Here's the code:

```
import java.awt.*;
import java.applet.Applet;

class FamousEquations extends Panel {
    Panel cards;
```

```
final static String EINSTEIN = "Einstein's most famous
    equation";
final static String NEWTON = "Newton's most famous equation";

public void init() {
    Panel   p;
    Panel   cp;
    Choice  c;

    setLayout(new BorderLayout());

    // This creates a choice box with two entries.
    cp = new Panel();
    c = new Choice();
    c.addItem(EINSTEIN);
    c.addItem(NEWTON);
    cp.add(c);
    add("North", cp);

    // We'll keep our cards in a panel.
    cards = new Panel();
    cards.setLayout(new CardLayout());

    p = new Panel();
    p.add(new Label("E=mc(squared)"));
    cards.add(EINSTEIN, p); // name the card

    p = new Panel();
    p.add(new Label("f=ma"));
    cards.add(NEWTON, p); // name the card so we can flip to it

    add("Center", cards);
    resize(200, 100);
}

public boolean action(Event evt, Object arg) {
    if (evt.target instanceof Choice) {
     ((CardLayout)cards.getLayout()).show(cards,(String)arg);
        return true;
    }
    return false;
}

public static void main(String args[]) {
    Frame f = new Frame("Famous Equations");
    FamousEquations fe = new FamousEquations();

    fe.init();

    f.add("Center", fe);
    f.pack();
    f.resize(f.preferredSize());
    f.show();
}
}
```

As you can see, we name the card (that is, the panel) when adding it to the CardLayout. When the user selects a new choice, we intercept that event and flip to the appropriately named card in the CardLayout.

GridBagLayout

The basic idea of a GridBagLayout is this: While components are basically arranged in a grid, each component can occupy more than one cell. GridBagLayouts are definitely the most complex way to arrange your UI using a layout manager, but they are also the most flexible.

To help a GridBagLayout figure out where and how to place different components, you use a GridBagConstraints object. This object contains a number of fields that you can set according to your preferences for where a particular component should be placed in the overall grid. There are quite a few settings in a GridBagConstraints object, though you can usually just use most of the default settings and set the one or two fields that really concern you. Your choices are presented next. You can control:

where in the overall grid to place a particular component—Use `gridx` and `gridy` to indicate a row and column at the upper left of the component's display area. Using `gridx=0` and `gridy=0` places the component in the upper left of the overall grid. If you specify `GridBagConstraints.RELATIVE` for either `gridx` or `gridy`, the new component will be added to the right of or below the previous component, as appropriate.

how many rows and columns in the overall grid a particular component will occupy—The fields `gridwidth` and `gridheight` determine the number of rows and columns assigned to a component. If you assign one of these fields the value `GridBagConstraints.REMAINDER`, the component you add will be the last one in its row or column, as appropriate.

whether or not to expand the component to fill its cell region—Use the `fill` field to specify `GridBagConstraints.NONE`, `GridBagConstraints.HORIZONTAL` to expand to the width of the component's display area, `GridBagConstraints.VERTICAL` to expand to the height of the component's display area, and `GridBagConstraints.BOTH` to expand both vertically and horizontally.

how much of a border should be allowed between the component and its cell boundaries—The fields `ipadx` and `ipady` indicate how much padding to add to the minimum size of the component.

the padding outside a component—The field `insets` defines the padding to place around the component within its display area.

an anchor point (or alignment) within a cell—Using the `anchor` field, you can place a component within its display region using the directions of the compass: `GridBagConstraints.NORTH`, `Grid-BagConstraints.NORTHWEST`, and so on. (Note that there are only eight compass points. You can't place a component north by northwest, for example.)

an indication of which cell to start with when laying out the components within the grid—Use the `weightx` and `weighty` fields to indicate which component the layout manager should start at when arranging them. You must specify at least one component in a row and one component in a column to let your GridBagLayout start somewhere and arrange your components as you intend.

While there are a lot of fields, in practice you don't have to set them all. Most of the time you can trust the defaults to do the right thing. (Remember, however, to at least set a `weightx` for each row and a `weighty` for each column.)

Using GridBagLayout

JavaWalker uses a GridBagLayout to arrange its user interface components in a panel. JavaWalker defines a Panel subclass called `JavaWalker-Panel` to organize its user interface elements. These elements consist of

- at the top, a label that says "Java Walker"
- below that, a label that says "Root:"
- to the right of this label, a text field for entering the root URL
- below this, four buttons: "Start", "Pause", "Resume", and "Close"
- below the four buttons, a list box for displaying the URLs found when walking the Web
- at the very bottom, a label for displaying status messages

In practice, one technique that works well is to create two GridBag-Constraints. The first contains the defaults. The second is used to maintain values to set the last component in each row. This is how the JavaWalkerPanel uses a GridBagLayout in the following code. This example shows how its constructor creates a nice-looking user interface using a GridBagLayout:

```java
class JavaWalkerPanel extends Panel {
    JavaWalker walker;      // The applet
    List       walkerList;  // This shows the URL hierarchy
    Thread     walkerThread;// The thread doing the searching
    Label      status;      // The status box for status messages
    int        urlIndex;    // The index of the current URL
    Button     pause;
    Button     resume;
    String     rootURLStr;
    TextField  rootTextField;
    JavaWalkerPanel (JavaWalker myWalker) {
        walker = myWalker;

        GridBagConstraints c = new GridBagConstraints ();
        GridBagConstraints endConst = new GridBagConstraints ();
        GridBagLayout gridbag = new GridBagLayout ();
        setLayout (gridbag);

        /* Constraints for the last component in a row.  */
        endConst.weightx = 1.0;
        endConst.fill = GridBagConstraints.HORIZONTAL;
        endConst.gridwidth = GridBagConstraints.REMAINDER;

        /* The applet label.  */
        Label label = new Label ("Java Walker", Label.LEFT);
        label.setFont (new Font ("Helvetica", Font.ITALIC, 24));
        endConst.insets = new Insets (4, 0, 4, 0);
        gridbag.setConstraints (label, endConst);
        add (label);

        /* The text field for entering the root URL.  */
        add (new Label ("Root:", Label.CENTER));
        rootTextField = new TextField ("");
        gridbag.setConstraints (rootTextField, endConst);
        add (rootTextField);

        /* The button control panel.  */
        Panel p = new Panel ();
        p.add (new Button ("Start"));
        p.add (pause = new Button ("Pause"));
        p.add (resume = new Button ("Resume"));
```

```
        p.add (new Button ("Close"));
        endConst.insets = new Insets (0, 0, 0, 0);
        gridbag.setConstraints (p, endConst);
        add (p);

        /* The list box displaying the URL hierarchy.  */
        walkerList = new List (8, false);
     walkerList.setFont (new Font ("Helvetica", Font.PLAIN, 10));
        endConst.insets = new Insets (2, 10, 2, 10);
        gridbag.setConstraints (walkerList, endConst);
        add (walkerList);

        /* The label for displaying status messages.  */
        status = new Label ("Enter a URL and click on Start.",
            Label.LEFT);
        status.setFont (new Font ("Times", Font.BOLD, 10));
        endConst.insets = new Insets (0, 10, 2, 10);
        gridbag.setConstraints (status, endConst);
        add (status);

        /* Initialize the components.  */
        pause.disable ();
        resume.disable ();
        setRootURL ("http://www.aw.com/devpress");
        rootTextField.setText (rootURLStr);
    }
    // ... additional methods
}
```

Implementing Your Own Layout Manager

To implement your own layout manager, you must supply behavior for the five methods defined by the LayoutManager interface:

1. `layoutContainer()` lays out the container in the specified panel. This method is your primary concern.

2. `addLayoutComponent()` adds a component to the layout given a name. (BorderLayouts, for example, use the names "North", "South", and so on.)

3. `minimumLayoutSize()` calculates the minimum size dimensions for the specified panel given the components in the specified parent container. This method returns a Dimension instance.

4. `preferredLayoutSize()` calculates the preferred size dimensions for the specified panel given the components in the

specified parent container. This method also returns a Dimension instance.

5. `removeLayoutComponent()` removes the specified component from the layout.

Implementors of a layout manager should consider the following two design issues:

1. Layout managers must know which components to arrange. To do this, they can either keep track of components themselves, such as in a hash table, or access the components in the parent container that's passed to them in `layoutContainer()`. For example, if the argument variable assigned to the container is named `parent`, the layout manager can determine the number of components in the container by using `parent.countComponents()`. The layout manager can then access an individual component by calling `parent.getComponent(number)`.

2. Since layout managers should be platform independent, they must make an extra effort to ensure they do not hard-code positions and coordinates. As mentioned previously, basing sizes on the current font is one way around monitor-specific pixel sizes.

Note that when a component is added to a container using `add()`, the container also adds the component to its layout manager. When the container receives `add(name, component)`, the container also dispatches `addLayoutComponent(name, component)` to its layout manager. That's how the BorderLayout knows, for example, to position an element in a particular region ("North", "South", and so on).

Low-Level Drawing

To use a graphics operation, you must be in possession of a Graphics object. The Graphics class describes methods for low-level drawing operations, such as the ability to render lines, polygons, images, and so on. To draw, you typically set the drawing color and then draw whatever it is you need.

If you override the `paint()` method for your component, the runtime will hand you a Graphics object for your component. This is definitely the easiest way to take advantage of graphics operations since Java will call your `paint()` method for you whenever your component should be redrawn (such as when the user resizes a window or the user closes a window that was overlapping your component).

Otherwise, if you're not in the `paint()` method and you do not have a Graphics object, you must find a way to get one. You can use a Component method called `getGraphics()` to acquire that component's Graphics instance. (If the component is not on the screen, `getGraphics()` returns null.)

The Pendulum application draws a circle and a line to represent the pendulum's weight and cord, respectively. The Weight class and the Cord class that make up the pendulum inherit from class Object (not class Component), so `getGraphics()` will not work on them. The Pendulum application, however, can still solve the problem of what Graphics instance to use. The primary Pendulum class is the applet, and this is where we want to draw the pendulum. You can force a component to repaint itself by calling its `repaint()` method. This causes the AWT to turn around and call your component's `paint()` method (Figure 13.13).

Every time the pendulum moves a little, the Pendulum applet calls `repaint()`. In the Pendulum applet's `paint()` method, the applet calls a new method called `draw()` that's defined for class Cord and class

Figure 13.13   AWT's paint() and repaint() methods

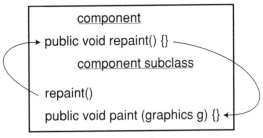

Weight. The applet passes `draw()` the Graphics instance the applet received in its `paint()` method. Here are the key portions of this code:

```
class Pendulum extends Applet implements Runnable {
    Thread  myThread;
    Weight  weight;
    Cord    cord;

    // ... various methods and other variables

    public void run() {
        while (myThread != null) {
            weight.swing();
            repaint();
        }
    }

    public void paint(Graphics g) {
        cord.draw(g);
        weight.draw(g);
    }
}

class Cord {
    // ... various methods and variables ...
    public void draw(Graphics g) {
        // ... draw the cord from the pivot to the weight ...
    }
}

class Weight {
    // ... various methods and variables ...
    public void draw(Graphics g) {
        // ... draw the weight at the end of the pendulum ...
    }
}
```

Colors

To set the color for drawing, you can take advantage of a bunch of predefined colors that are maintained by `static` variables in the Color class. These colors include white, light gray, gray, dark gray, black, red, pink, orange, yellow, green, magenta, cyan, and blue.

You can also define your own custom colors. To do so, you must set the red, green, and blue values for your color when you call Color's constructor. Color also defines routines to return a lighter or darker version of your color and also supplies conversions between {hue, saturation, brightness} and {red, green, blue} values.

Some Examples of Low-Level Graphics

Drawing a line is easy. Just indicate the two end points and you're done. Here's how the cord part of the pendulum draws itself:

```
public static final Color   CORD_COLOR     = Color.black;
public static final int      CORD_PIVOT_X  = 300;
public static final int      CORD_PIVOT_Y  = 20;

Pendulum p;
public void draw(Graphics g) {
   g.setColor(CORD_COLOR);
      g.drawLine(CORD_PIVOT_X, CORD_PIVOT_Y, p.weight.xpos,
p.weight.ypos);
}
```

The cord defines constants to keep track of the end point that's the pivot and the color to be used when it's drawn. The cord refers back to the Pendulum instance to find the current position for the weight to know where to draw the other end point of the line.

The weight, in turn, draws itself as a circle. To draw an oval shape, you can use the `fillOval()` method, which takes `x`, `y`, `width`, and `height` as parameters.

The coordinates for everything in Java (that is, for all of its components and graphics primitives) are defined with (0,0) located in the upper left. If we were to draw a circle with the `x` and `y` values both set to 10 and the `width` and `height` values also both set to 10, the circle's center would be at (15,15). That is, the `x` and `y` values in `fillOval()` define the upper left of the circle, not its center.

So, to draw the circle centered at (x,y) rather than using (x,y) as the top left of the circle's boundary, we must offset the top-left coordinate for the circle by the circle's radius, which is just what the Pendulum's Weight class does when it draws:

```
public static final Color   WT_COLOR     = Color.blue;
public static final int      WT_DIAMETER = 50;
public int                    xpos;
public int                    ypos;
```

```
public void draw(Graphics g) {
   int radius = WT_DIAMETER/2;
   g.setColor(WT_COLOR);
   g.fillOval(xpos - radius, ypos - radius, WT_DIAMETER,
WT_DIAMETER);
}
```

This works wonderfully well. However, on a slow system, the pendulum can look a little shaky and seem to flicker. This occurs because the `repaint()` method requests that the AWT dirty the entire component. The window that contains the pendulum, however, can be much bigger than the pieces of the pendulum that actually must be repainted, resulting in a lot of repainting of the background that's unnecessary.

Rather than using `repaint()` without any parameters, you can pass `repaint()` the bounds of the region that should be repainted. The small amount of time required to calculate the bounds really needing repainting makes the Pendulum applet run much more smoothly.

More About Events

The Pendulum applet allows a user to interact with it. When a user holds down the mouse button, the user can drag the weight at the end of the pendulum. This causes the cord to stretch and contract but remain taut between the pivot and the weight. When the user lets go, the pendulum begins swinging again from its new location.

To track mouse movements, the Pendulum applet must know when certain events have occurred. Rather than overriding `handleEvent()` and trying to detect mouse events, the Pendulum applet lets the default `handleEvent()` code do its thing. The AWT components will handle this method by calling more detailed event methods, if appropriate. In the case of mouse movements, AWT defines a number of events that correspond to particular mouse events. The Pendulum applet takes advantage of these to override

- `mouseDown()`, to stop the pendulum from swinging

```
/** Called when the mouse goes down. Stop swinging. */
public boolean mouseDown(Event e, int x, int y) {
   freeze = true;
   return false; // pass this event up the window hierarchy
}
```

■ `mouseDrag()`, to redraw the weight and the cord appropriately

```
/** Reset the weight to this position as the user drags it
around. */
    public boolean mouseDrag(Event e, int x, int y) {
        weight.newPosition(x, y);
        return false; // pass this event up the window hierarchy
    }
```

■ `mouseUp()`, to start the pendulum swinging again

```
/** Called when the mouse goes up. Start swinging again. */
    public boolean mouseUp(Event e, int x, int y) {
        freeze = false;
        return false; // pass this event up the window hierarchy
    }
```

A couple of screenshots that show the pendulum stretching to follow the user's mouse are provided in Figure 13.14 and 13.15.

You can use similar techniques in your own applications and applets. That is, rather than always overriding `handleEvent()`, you can

Figure 13.14 Making a very large pendulum

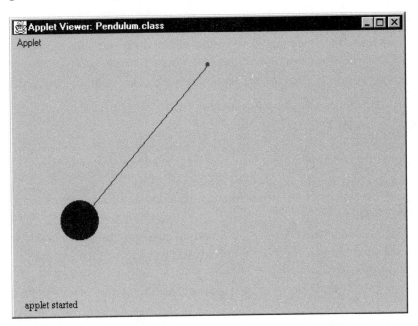

Figure 13.15 Making a very small pendulum

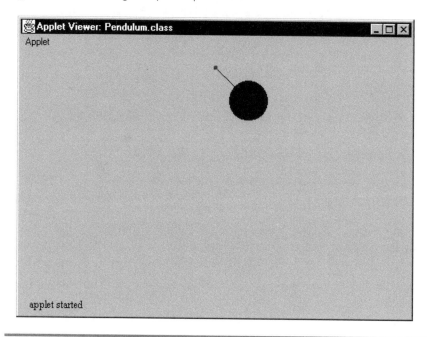

override the methods that correspond to the more specific events of interest to you. You can also look for keyboard events such as `keyUp()` and `keyDown()`. These events also indicate the key that was pressed.

Other AWT Classes

Some other useful classes in the AWT library are as follows:

- Canvas can be subclassed to create your own user interface components.
- Checkbox implements the standard checkbox user interface item.
- CheckboxGroup groups checkboxes together to create exclusive choices.
- FileDialog displays a file selection dialog to allow the user to pick a file.
- Font creates font objects based on the style you specify.

- Menu defines individual components for a menubar.
- Menubar implements the specific platform's version of a menu bar.
- MenuItem represents a choice in a menu that you can enable and disable.
- TextArea creates a region for displaying text.

■ FILES WITH JAVA.IO

The package java.io provides classes that act as handles to file system nodes (that is, to files and directories). These classes allow you to read and write streams of bytes. The FileBrowser application shows how to work with files in the file system.

File and Directory Handles

The FileBrowser application uses an instance of the File class to obtain a handle on the current directory. The code is straightforward:

```
File cwd = new File(".");
```

The File class can also provide a level of abstraction when dealing with file handles. For example, a File instance can return the file separator for a particular file system, so you don't have to worry about whether it's a "/", "\", or ":".

Listing Files

Once we have a handle to a directory, we can ask for the list of files in the directory simply by using the File's list() method. Since this method might throw an I/O exception if it has trouble getting the files, we have to be prepared to catch this:

```
try {
    file_list = cwd.list();
} catch (java.io.IOException x) {
    System.out.println("couldn't open .");
    return;
}
```

Reading Files

Once the user has selected a file from the list, the user can click the view button to display this file in a separate window. FileBrowser creates a new instance of a Frame subclass called `FileViewer`, passing File-Viewer's constructor the name of the file to display. FileViewer takes care of reading the file into a list and adding the list as a subview of its window hierarchy.

The next example shows how to use the FileInputStream and DataInputStream classes to read the contents of a file—that is, how to

- create a FileInputStream instance given a string representing the file name
- create a DataInputStream instance to open the file for reading
- call `readLine()` to read a line from the DataInputStream instance (that is, from the file)

If the line is read from the file without errors, it's added to a list that we'll use to present the file's contents. This list will be added to the File-Viewer as a subview:

```
class FileViewer extends Frame {

    public FileViewer(String file_name) {
        String str;
        List text_listing = new List();
        FileInputStream file_stream;

        try {
            file_stream = new FileInputStream(file_name);
        } catch (java.io.FileNotFoundException x) {
            return;
        }

        DataInputStream contents = new DataInputStream(file_stream);

        try {
            str = contents.readLine();
            if (str == null) {
                text_listing.addItem("No errors encountered");
            } else while (str != null) {
                text_listing.addItem(str);
                str = contents.readLine();
            }
```

```
        } catch (java.io.IOException x) {
            text_listing.addItem("View interrupted");
        }

        add("Center", text_listing);
        // ... add more UI elements and display this Frame

    }
}
```

Note that we have to be prepared to handle two exceptions. First, when obtaining a handle to the file, we have to get ready to catch an exception that Java might throw (for example, if Java cannot find the file name matching the string we pass to the constructor). Second, when reading from the file, we should be ready to catch any I/O exceptions that might occur.

JavaWalker also uses an instance of class DataInputStream when it reads the HTML file over the Web. You'll see how JavaWalker does this in the next section on Internet protocols.

■ INTERNET PROGRAMMING USING JAVA.NET

The package `java.net` provides classes that assist with communicating over the Internet. You can deal with Internet protocols at two distinct levels. You can stay at the more abstract level of Universal Resource Locators (URLs) and Internet addresses, or you can get down and dirty and play with socket I/O and packet data.

The JavaWalker application accesses information on the Web strictly by using URLs. After reviewing how JavaWalker does its thing, we'll take a look at JavaTalker and see how to use sockets in your own applications.

High-Level Communication

You can implement fairly sophisticated Web programs simply by sticking with Java's URL class. The URL class is, in fact, the only class JavaWalker needs from the net package to go on a walking tour of the Web. Here's the primary algorithm for JavaWalker:

1. Determine the URL to find (starting with the given root URL if we're just starting our tour).
2. Create a URL instance from the URL's String.
3. Open a URL resource by creating a stream.
4. Read the resource using this stream.
5. Parse the data from the stream, looking for more URLs.
6. If there are more URLs, pick one and go back to step 2.

We start the implementation of this algorithm by creating a new buffer to place the data we will read over the Web:

```
StringBuffer buffer = new StringBuffer ();
```

We set the current URL (either the root URL the user supplies or a new URL we've found during our walk):

```
walkerPanel.setCurrentURL (urlStr, depth);
```

We then create a URL instance out of the String representing the URL. We open the URL as a stream and read it, line by line, until there's no more data:

```
try {
    URL url = new URL (urlStr);
    DataInputStream stream =
        new DataInputStream (url.openStream ());
    String str;

    while ((str = stream.readLine ()) != null) {
        buffer.append (str);
    }
```

Notice how straightforward the URL class makes accessing data over the Web. All we have to do is use its openStream() method, and we can create a new DataInputStream object to read the Internet resource. We read the data using readLine() (which was first discussed in Chapter 6), and, just like that, the Web page has been accessed over the Web and read into a buffer.

Before JavaWalker parses the data in the input buffer and looks for more URLs, it saves the URL it just visited so that it does not double back on itself and parse the same location again if another Web page makes reference to it. The `urlsVisited` variable refers to a hash table:

```
urlsVisited.put (urlStr, new Integer (depth));
```

JavaWalker then parses the buffer in search of a String that begins with "http:" and ends with ".html". If JavaWalker finds any new URLs, they will be added to the queue of URLs still to be explored. JavaWalker does this by first creating a new instance of its URLParser class with the data it read in over the Web. After displaying a status message, we call the URLParser's `parse()` method, which looks through this HTML file as described earlier in this chapter (see the discussion on String methods):

```
URLParser parser = new URLParser (buffer.toString ());
walkerPanel.reportStatus ("Parsing " + urlStr + "...");
Queue q = parser.parse ();
```

Low-Level Communication

While JavaWalker shows URLs in action, JavaTalker is a great example of performing some low-level communication. JavaTalker works by following this algorithm:

1. Parse the command line arguments to determine whether this invocation of JavaTalker should run as a client or server application, which Internet host to connect to, and which port on the host to connect to.
2. If JavaTalker is run as a server, wait for a connection to arrive on the specified socket. Figure 13.16 shows the application waiting for a connection to be made.
3. If JavaTalker is run as a client, try to establish the connection to the server. Figure 13.17 shows what the user sees when the connection is made.
4. Once a connection is established, spawn two threads. A writer thread first opens an input stream from the socket and waits for

Figure 13.16 JavaTalker as a server: waiting until someone connects

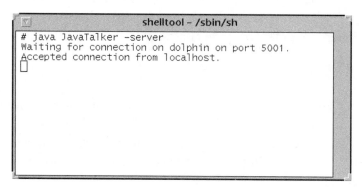

data to arrive. A reader thread opens an input stream from the standard input and waits for data to arrive.

5. When new data arrives for the reader, direct it to the socket (Figure 13.18). When new data arrives for the writer, direct it to the standard output (Figure 13.19).

All this is done in just a page or two of Java code. Pretty cool!

Here's how JavaTalker sets itself up to be a server (discussion of this code follows):

Figure 13.17 JavaTalker as a client: trying to connect to the server

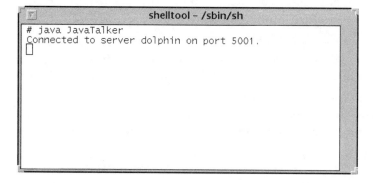

Figure 13.18 Sending a message via the Internet

```
┌─────────────────────────────────────────────────────┐
│ ▣            shelltool – /sbin/sh                    │
├─────────────────────────────────────────────────────┤
│ # java JavaTalker                                   │
│ Connected to server dolphin on port 5001.           │
│ Happy New Year!                                     │
│ ☐                                                   │
│                                                     │
│                                                     │
│                                                     │
│                                                     │
│                                                     │
│                                                     │
└─────────────────────────────────────────────────────┘
```

```java
public void server () {
    /*
     * As a server, we create a server socket bound to the
     * specified port, wait for a connection, and then spawn
     * the reader and writer threads.
     */
    try {
        InetAddress serverAddr = InetAddress.getByName (null);

        System.out.println ("Waiting for connection on " +
                            serverAddr.getHostName () +
                            " on port " + port + ".");

        ServerSocket serverSock = new ServerSocket (port, 50);
        sock = serverSock.accept ();
```

Figure 13.19 Receiving the message and replying

```
┌─────────────────────────────────────────────────────┐
│ ▣            shelltool – /sbin/sh                    │
├─────────────────────────────────────────────────────┤
│ # java JavaTalker –server                           │
│ Waiting for connection on dolphin on port 5001.     │
│ Accepted connection from localhost.                 │
│ Happy New Year!                                     │
│ Thanks! The fireworks at the Space Needle were great!│
│ ☐                                                   │
│                                                     │
│                                                     │
│                                                     │
│                                                     │
└─────────────────────────────────────────────────────┘
```

```
            System.out.println ("Accepted connection from " +
                sock.getInetAddress() .getHostName () + ".");

            new JavaTalkerWriter (this).start ();
            new JavaTalkerReader (this).start ();

        } // ... catch any exceptions ...
    }
```

First, the `static` method `getByName()` in InetAddress retrieves the network address for the indicated host. If the String specifying the host is not defined (that is, if it's set to `null`, as it is in this example), then `getByName()` returns the network address for the local machine. This is what we want since we want to be the server.

The method `getHostName()` returns a String representing the host name for the Internet address. We use this method to tell the user what's happening. (The variable `port` will contain the default port set in the code, or the user can specify the port as part of JavaTalker's command line arguments.)

Next, we create a new socket for the server. We pass the Server-Socket constructor the port number and set how long we'll wait to establish the connection.

Then, it's a waiting game. The server socket's `accept()` method blocks the program's execution until a connection is made. Once the connection is established, `accept()` returns information in a Socket instance about who connected with us. We use the Socket's `getInetAddress()` method to get the InetAddress instance representing the client that made the connection and then use `getHostName()` to show this to the user.

Next, we start two threads, one to read incoming data and one to write outgoing data. Before we look at these threads, consider how JavaTalker sets itself up when run as a client (again, a discussion follows):

```
    public void client () {
        /*
         * As a client, we create a socket bound to the specified
         * port, connect to the specified host, and then spawn the
         * reader and writer threads.
         */
        try {
            InetAddress serverAddr = InetAddress.getByName (host);
            sock = new Socket (serverAddr.getHostName (), port,
true);
```

```
System.out.println ("Connected to server " +
                serverAddr.getHostName () +
                " on port " + sock.getPort () + ".");

    new JavaTalkerWriter (this).start ();
    new JavaTalkerReader (this).start ();

    } // ... catch any exceptions ...
  }
}
```

This code is similar to, though slightly simpler than, the server code. When we create the socket for the client, we indicate we want to connect to the host the user passed in as a command line argument (otherwise, this code establishes a connection to the same machine, which is useful for testing). We also specify the port and use a Boolean value to indicate this socket is to be used as a stream.

If we connect okay, we display the server information and start up the threads for chatting, and we're off!

Here's the `run()` method for the thread that reads data from the standard input and writes it to the socket:

```
public synchronized void run () {
    try {
        DataInputStream userIn =
            new DataInputStream (System.in);
        DataOutputStream remoteOut =

            new DataOutputStream (talker.sock.getOutputStream ());

        while (true) {
            talker.busyWait (userIn);
            remoteOut.writeChars (userIn.readLine () + '\n');
        }
    } // ... catch any exceptions ...
}
```

We create a data input stream based on the standard input and open a stream for writing to the socket. We then wait for new input. Our `busyWait()` method loops forever until data is available:

```
try {
    while (inStream.available () <= 0) {
        Thread.currentThread ().sleep (100);
    }
```

Once data arrives, we fall out of the loop and write the data to the socket.

Here's the `run()` method for the writer thread (this code should start to look familiar to you):

```
public synchronized void run () {
    try {
        DataInputStream remoteIn =
        new DataInputStream (talker.sock.getInputStream ());
         while (true) {
            talker.busyWait (remoteIn);
            System.out.println (remoteIn.readLine ());
        }
    } // ... catch any exceptions ...
}
```

We open an input stream for the socket and wait for data to arrive. When it does, we write it to the screen.

Both this package and JavaWalker give you a sense of how Java's net package handles many of the details concerning Internet programming for you. This allows your program to stay at a more abstract level and concentrate on the basic logic, data flow, and user interactions rather than the specifics of Internet protocols.

■ UTILITIES IN JAVA.UTIL

The package `java.util` provides all sorts of great classes to help perform standard programming chores. These classes include dates, vectors, hash tables, and random number generators.

Dates

The Date class makes dealing with dates and times a snap. To create an instance of class Date that's basically a time stamp (that is, that's set to the current date and time), simply use the Date constructor without arguments:

```
Date timeStamp = Date();
```

Date classes work with years after 1900. Months are defined in the range 0 to 11. Days in a month range from 1 to 31. Dates are very good about always staying consistent. If you add more days to a Date than there are days in that month, the Date instance will normalize the date appropriately by carrying the days into the months and years columns as necessary.

Dates are based on the current *epoch*. The current epoch began not on some date that you'd at first think of, such as when Neil Armstrong landed on the moon or when the last ice age ended, but when disco began (0 hours on January 1, 1970). Keeping track of the milliseconds since the current epoch is fine as long as Java uses a 64-bit integer, which it does. Unfortunately, this number will overflow before the disco era returns, in the year 292280995.

You can use a variety of constructors to create a Date instance set to a particular date and time. For example, to create a date on October 27, 1961, you can write

```
Date d = Date(61, 9, 27);
```

(Remember, months are 0 based and days are 1 based.)

If you know the hours, minutes, and seconds, you can throw those in, too. So, for 2:15 in the afternoon on the date just given, you can write

```
Date d = Date(61, 9, 27, 14, 15, 0);
```

(Note that hours range between 0 and 23.)

There are a number of convenient methods to parse a string containing a date and to retrieve or set particular values in a date (the hour, month, and so on). You can get the time in milliseconds since the beginning of the current epoch. You can ask whether a particular date falls before or after another date. Dates also can return Strings representing their values and can be adjusted for local time zones.

Vectors

Vectors allow you to define collections of objects. The Vector class defines all sorts of useful methods to set and get particular elements, test if the Vector is empty, and determine the size and allocated storage of a Vector. Subclasses of Vector can also access elements by using an array notation.

Vectors handle storage intelligently. Rather than always allocating new storage whenever a new element is added to the Vector instance, Vectors increase in size by chunks.

Both JavaWalker and TownHall use the Vector class to create a queue. The `util` package does define a stack, but it lacks a queue (as of version 1.0). In a stack, the last item in is the first item to come out. In a queue, the first item in is the first item out (similarly, the last item in is the last item out).

With our home-grown Queue class, you can add a new element to the queue. Doing so inserts the element in location 0, pushing back all the other elements. You can also access an element from the queue. Retrieving an element grabs the oldest element in the queue, removes it from the queue, and returns the item:

```
class Queue extends Vector {
  public void enqueue (Object o) {
    insertElementAt (o, 0);
  }

  public Object dequeue () {
    Object o = lastElement ();
    removeElementAt (size () - 1);
    return o;
  }
}
```

Hash Tables

JavaWalker uses the `util` package to define a hash table. A hash table allows you to store objects using `put()` and access objects using `get()`. Objects are stored and retrieved based on a key. The object used as the key must implement two methods:

1. `hashCode()` is used to obtain the key.
2. `equals()` is used to compare keys.

Class Object already supplies default behavior for these methods. Class Object provides a unique number for each object in the Java runtime environment. You can override these methods if you like. For example, class String overrides these methods to return its own value and to compare strings. The Date class also overrides these methods and tests for equal dates between two different date instances.

JavaWalker uses a hash table to keep track of whether it has already included a particular Web page destination in its display. This saves the link trail from displaying loops and redundancies and so provides a cleaner display.

The `put()` method takes two parameters. The first is the object to be used as the key; the second is the object to store. JavaWalker is interested in finding out if a particular URL has already been included in its display of destination pages. So, it uses the URL's string as the key. For a value, JavaWalker creates an Integer instance out of the depth at which this URL is found. Though JavaWalker, as it is currently written, has no need to do this, it could later find the depth of a particular URL by using the following code:

```
Integer depth = urlsVisited.get(urlStr);
```

where `urlStr` is a String instance containing the Web page's URL. As it is, JavaWalker only needs to remember the URL, so it executes the following code:

```
urlsVisited.put(urlStr, new Integer(depth));
```

When JavaWalker wants to know if a URL was already included in its display, it checks the hash table for a key matching the URL string:

```
urlsVisited.containsKey(urlStr)
```

This will yield `true` or `false`, depending on whether the URL is already in the hash table or not.

Note that the URLs could not really be maintained in a Vector instance. While you can check to see whether a vector contains a given object, these objects are not stored by key value. So, different String instances representing the same URL would be different objects in a vector. However, Strings containing identical text use identical hash codes, which produce the desired effects.

Random Number Generators

The `util` package contains a class called `Random`, which allows you to define a random number generator. To get the most mileage out of this class, it's often good to seed the random number generator when you create an instance of this class. To do so, you can pass it a `long` value as the seed:

```
Random r = Random(mySeed);
```

What makes a good seed? There are many possibilities, but here are two that should work fairly well:

1. Use the hashcode for an object. For example, you can write

```
Random r = Random(hashCode(myObject));
```

2. Use the time in milliseconds since the beginning of the current epoch (January 1, 1970). To get this time in milliseconds, you need to create a Date instance. For example, you can write

```
Random r = Random(Date().getTime());
```

The TownHall application creates a random number generator using the preceding technique to seed what the good citizens will say. You can reset the seed at any time using `setSeed()`. You can also grab the next random number of a particular type using `nextInt()`, `next-Long()`, `nextFloat()`, `nextDouble()`, or `nextGaussian()`. Integer values are between the minimum and the maximum for that data type. Floating-point values are between 0.0 and 1.0. Gaussian values have a mean of 0.0 and a standard deviation of 1.0.

The TownHall application requests the next `int` value from the random number generator, performs a modulo operation with the length of the array that contains the choices, and then takes the absolute value of this:

```
Math.abs(r.nextInt())%nouns.length
```

The result is a value between 0 and `nouns.length`. The TownHall application then uses this value to access an element from the `nouns[]` array.

■ SUMMARY

This chapter described how Java's packages assisted in developing some powerful applications. By building from the functionality already provided by Java, these applications were created much more easily than if all the code had to be written from scratch.

This chapter covered important aspects of Java's packages in depth. More information was provided on Java's graphics and layout capabilities, its file handling, how to interact with the Internet, and how to use some convenient utility classes. You should now have a grasp of what's there for you, where to look, and how to take advantage of Java's classes to create your own advanced applications.

■ WHAT'S NEXT?

In Chapter 14, we'll follow up with another important package, `java.applet`. This package makes it possible to create applications that run over the Web. You were introduced to writing applets in Chapter 8. The next chapter provides many more details on how to write Java code that users can access via a Web browser.

14

Writing for the Web

Chapter 8 already provided an overview of taking a Java application and turning it into an applet that runs over the Web. Chapter 14 explores some of the details that we haven't yet talked about. There are a number of methods that are useful for interacting with the Web and the Web browser in which your applet is running. There are also a few special considerations you should be aware of when running in the Web as opposed to a stand-alone environment.

■ A QUICK REVIEW

Applet Subclass

Java-enabled Web browsers expect to interact with a subclass of Applet. All Applet subclasses must be declared as `public`. You can override certain messages in your Applet subclass that the Java runtime calls at critical times in your Applet's life.

Applet Life Cycle

There are four methods you will care about most:

1. The `init()` method is called when your Applet is first downloaded.
2. `start()` is invoked when the user turns to your page.
3. The browser calls your `stop()` method when the user leaves or discards your page.
4. If the page was discarded, the browser also calls `destroy()`.

Window Hierarchy

Your applet runs in the window displaying the Web page that's provided by the Web browser. At first, your applet is treated just like any other display element; the browser flows the rest of the Web page around the space required by your applet. If the user has indicated that the browser should run applets, the browser verifies the byte codes and then calls the applet's `init()` and `start()` methods to bring the applet to life.

Embedding an Applet in an HTML Page

To signal the browser that your Web page contains an applet, you must use the `<applet>` tag. Place any arguments that your applet accepts between the `<applet>` and `</applet>` tags as name/value pairs. You'll set a `width` value and a `height` value within the `<applet>` tag to give the applet a default size (your applet can override this size in its `init()` method if it wishes):

```
<title>Hello, Applet!</title>
<hr>
<applet code=HelloApplet.class width=600 height=300>
</applet>
<hr>
<a href="HelloApplet.java">The source.</a>
```

The next two sections explain how to pass other parameters to your applet as well.

■ THE APPLET CLASS AND THE APPLETCONTEXT INTERFACE

Applets and AppletContexts define methods that allow applets and browsers to interact. For example, you can use a method defined by AppletContext to tell the browser to display a particular Web page. You can also perform many Web-specific actions through simple method calls to your applet.

Applet

Class Applet defines a number of methods for interacting with resources on the Web. For example, you can obtain a sound file or a graphic image just by specifying its URL:

```
AudioClip ac = getAudioClip(targetURL);
Image i = getImage(targetURL);
```

If you'd like to let the user hear the sound clip, you can play it with a simple method call:

```
play(ac);
```

If you need to find a resource relative to the applet, you can find out the URL for the applet:

```
URL u = getCodeBase();
```

You can also find out the URL of the document in which the applet is embedded:

```
URL u = getDocumentBase();
```

There's an interesting method called `getParameterInfo()` that you might want to think about overriding for your applet. The intent of `getParameterInfo()` is to provide a way to get at parameters and values that are important in your applet. This method returns an array of String arrays—that is, `String[][]`. The array has three columns and any number of rows. The three columns define the name of the parameter, its type, and a comment about what it is.

For example, you can override the `getParameterInfo()` method for the JavaWalker applet discussed in the previous chapter. You might return information that relates to the first Web page from which to start walking the Web:

```
String[][] getParameterInfo() {
    String params = {{"Address", "String", "start page"}};
    return params;
}
```

Related to this is a method called `getParameter()` that you can use in conjunction with passing parameters to your applet. You'll see how to use this method in the next section.

AppletContext

If you want your applet to be able to interact with its environment, your applet needs to get a handle to the context in which the applet is running:

```
AppletContext ac = getAppletContext();
```

This context is typically the Web browser, which, in a Java-enabled browser, is defined using a class that implements the AppletContext interface. Once you have an AppletContext instance, you can interact with the browser.

You can acquire a handle to another applet on the current Web page if you can name it. Applet names can be assigned by using a `name` parameter. Once you have the applet, you might see whether it is currently running by calling its `isActive()` method. You can even `start()` or `stop()` the applet if you'd like to, and you can see what parameters are set for it.

If you dispatch `showDocument()` to the applet context (that is, to the browser), you can change the Web page it's showing by passing it a new URL. (Of course, if your applet is on the original page, your applet is likely to stop running since it will receive the `stop()` method when the browser turns away from the applet's page.)

■ PASSING VALUES TO AN APPLET

All you have to do to pass a value to your applet is specify an attribute name and a value for the attribute between the `<applet>` and `</applet>` tags. Here's an example:

```
<applet code=Sundae.class height=400 width=200>
<param name=icecream value="vanilla" name=sauce value="hot fudge">
</applet>
```

Then, inside your applet's code, you can determine the value of a parameter by using the `getParameter()` method:

```
String flavor = getParameter("icecream");
String topping = getParameter("sauce");
```

One particularly cool thing you can do with parameters is to pass in the name of a class you'd like to use within your applet. Java defines a method for working with classes by name that you can use to instantiate a class passed to the applet as a String. For example, if you have HTML tags that look like this

```
<applet code=MyApplet.class height=200 width=200>
<param name=myClass value="Astronaut">
</applet>
```

you can grab the class name in the code by using `getParameter()` in the usual way:

```
String name = getParameter("myClass");
```

Then, using a static method in the Class class, you can find this new class and instantiate it (the class is loaded over your Internet connection from the same host as the applet if the class doesn't already exist on the user's computer):

```
MyClass buzzLightyear = Class.forName(name).newInstance();
```

■ SPECIAL CONSIDERATIONS

Threads

When the user turns away from the Web page containing your applet, the browser will dispatch `stop()` to your applet. If you're running any threads, you should take this opportunity to stop them. This is particularly relevant if your thread happens to be painting on the screen; when your applet is no longer displayed, you don't want to keep on painting!

The example given later in the section on animation shows how you can respond to applet life-cycle methods to start and stop your applet threads at the appropriate times.

Images

It's often convenient to keep images on your Web server either in the same directory as the Web page on which the images will appear or collected into a subdirectory. Either way, you'll need to find the images relative to the current Web page.

When you first initialize your applet, you can retrieve the images from the server by finding them relative to your HTML document using the applet method `getDocumentBase()`. For example, you can write

```
public class ImageApplet extends Applet {
    Image image;
    public void init() {
        image = getImage(getDocumentBase(), "gifs/bluehorse.gif");
    }

    // fill the applet's window with the image:
    public void paint (Graphics g) {
        Rectangle r = bounds();
        g.drawImage(image, 0, 0, rect.width, rect.height, this);
    }
}
```

Use one of the four overloaded `drawImage()` methods defined by Graphics to draw an image. For each method, the last argument passed to `drawImage()` is an instance of ImageObserver. The role in life for an ImageObserver is to assist with drawing images that are downloaded over the Web. In particular, `getImage()` returns immediately, not waiting around for the image to download. If the image is in the process of being downloaded, the image observer automatically detects when new data is available, and the image is drawn incrementally until it is fully rendered. Applets automatically know how to be image observers; you don't have to write any special code to get this behavior.

Animation

The basic idea behind creating an animation in Java is to present a sequence of images in rapid succession. You can loop continuously through your images, or you can step through them once and then halt the animation on the last frame. Here are two methods that handle advancing to the next frame and painting the current image in the sequence:

```
public class AnimationApplet extends Applet {
    private int   currentFrame = 0;
    private int   currentImage;
    Image[]       images;
    int           xloc = 100;
    int           yloc = 100;

    // ... the usual applet methods ...

    public void advance() {
        if (currentImage == image.length)
            currentImage = 0;
        else
            currentImage++;
    }

    public void paint(Graphics g) {
        Image image = images[currentImage];
        g.drawImage(image, xloc, yloc, this);
        advance();
    }

    // ... more code to follow ...
}
```

(This example doesn't show obtaining the images over the Internet, which was illustrated when we acquired an image to paint in the preceding section.)

We still need to cycle through the images. When we do, we must make certain that the images don't whip by in the blink of an eye. To slow things down a bit, it's necessary to insert some downtime into your animation sequence.

Before you jump in and do this, note that you don't want to end up putting your entire applet to sleep, because end users will then have to wait to interact with your applet. One solution is to create a thread, implement the Runnable interface, and use the thread to trigger the animation sequence. Now, you can put your thread to sleep without abandoning your user:

```
public class AnimationApplet extends Applet implements Runnable {
   Thread sequencer;

   public void init() {
      sequencer = new Thread(this);
   }

   public void start() {
      if (sequencer.isAlive())
         sequencer.resume();
      else
         sequencer.start();
   }

   public void stop() {
      sequencer.suspend();
   }

   public void destroy() {
      sequencer.stop();
   }

   // ... more to follow ...
```

So far, this implements the four life-cycle methods that your applet should respond to when it defines threads for which it provides a `run()` method. The preceding code creates a thread when the applet is first initialized and stops the thread when the applet is discarded by the browser. When the user turns to the page or turns away from the page, the thread is started, resumed, or suspended, as appropriate.

Now, for the proof of the pudding:

```
// ... continued from above ...

public void run() {
   while(true) {
      repaint();
      Thread.sleep(750); // sleep for 3/4 of a second
   }
}
```

The static method defined by Thread causes the currently executing thread to go to sleep for the specified number of milliseconds. The currently executing thread is defined by the `sequencer` instance variable. So, while we halt the animation process, we don't halt the rest of the applet. Our `run()` method loops forever, repainting and waiting a small amount of time between frames.

One useful technique for making animation sequences paint smoothly is to first draw them offscreen. Then, after the system has handled all the chores of rendering the image (determining color, size, and mapping the image to the specific device on which the user is viewing the applet), the image is copied to the screen all at once. This can help eliminate any flickering the user might see and make the animation much nicer to watch.

To create an offscreen image, you can use the method `createImage()`, defined in the Component class, to create an image of a given dimension:

```
Image offscreen = createImage(width, height);
```

Then, when you want to work with this offscreen image, you can obtain a graphics context to it in the usual way, by calling its `getGraphics()` method:

```
Graphics context = offscreen.getGraphics();
```

Sounds

You can download sounds using the applet method `getAudioClip()`. Once you have a sound clip, you can either play it once or play it continuously as background music or sounds for your Web page.

To play a sound clip once, use its `play()` method. To play it continuously, invoke its `loop()` method. To silence it, call its `stop()` method. Note that you might want to be sure to call `stop()` when the user leaves the Web page so that the sound turns off when the user is no longer viewing your page!

One other note: You can play more than one sound file at once. Java will play a composite of the sounds produced by the multiple audio files.

Standard Output

Just because you're running an applet doesn't mean you won't see the results of any `System.out.println()` calls. The standard output will most likely still be available as a shell window in Unix or a DOS window in Windows 95.

Security Issues

Since the Java runtime attempts to keep code from damaging the user's environment, not all of Java's capabilities are available to applets. In particular, the following restrictions might be applied to the applets a user runs in a Web browser:

1. File I/O is likely to be restricted. Users might set the security in their browsers to restrict access to files in their local environment. This might, for example, disable an application such as the File-Browser if it is turned into an applet and distributed over the Web.
2. Accessing URLs might be restricted to the host on which the applet resides. This might preclude applications such as Java-Walker, which hops from server to server as it walks the Web.
3. Native methods (described in Appendix C) are inherently dependent on the platform for which they're compiled and so might not execute on a particular user's platform. In addition, Java applications that depend on native methods forgo Java's built-in security. Browsers might refuse to run native methods within Java's secure environment since C code can bypass Java's security measures.

User Interface Changes

You may want to present different options to the user depending on whether your code is being run as an applet on the Web or as a stand-alone application. You can create two different versions of your software, or you can detect in which environment your code is running. You'll know if your code was initiated by the Java interpreter because your `main()` routine will be called.

Figure 14.1 JavaWalker as an application

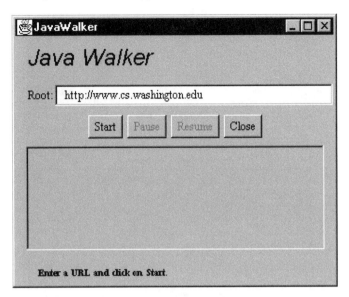

When JavaWalker is run as an application, it presents a button that allows the user to dismiss the application (Figure 14.1). The close button makes a System call to `exit()`, which causes the application to terminate.

In a browser, calls to `exit()` are ignored. When JavaWalker is run as a stand-alone, `main()` calls the UI construction code with a Boolean set to `true`. Otherwise, this button will not appear (Figure 14.2).

■ SUMMARY

This chapter highlighted the primary issues you'll need to take into account when developing Java applications that run over the Web. For the most part, you can use all the same features you've learned about in this book to write fun, useful, powerful Java applications for the Internet. There are some special considerations, such as stopping threads, retrieving image and sound resources, and security issues, but otherwise, it's business as usual. So, be creative and let the world see the finest applications you can develop!

Figure 14.2   JavaWalker as an applet

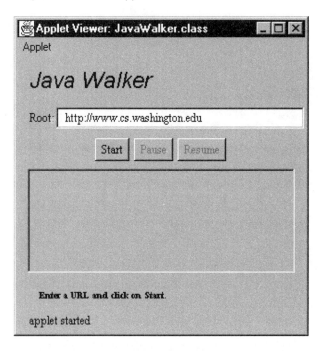

■ WHAT'S NEXT?

This book offered you a view on the Java language that took into account your hard-earned knowledge of programming. Having read this book, you've taken the first step in a journey that will lead to dazzling, multitasking, error-free programs running over the Web—and in other environments as well. Good luck and have fun in all your future programming endeavors!

PART IV

Appendices

The appendices provide the following information:

Appendix A: Compiling and Running Java Applications: This appendix describes the platform-specific details for compiling and executing Java applications using the Java Developer's Kit available from Sun Microsystems.

Appendix B: Source Code: This appendix presents the complete source listing to the applications that have been discussed and presented in part throughout this book.

Appendix C: Combining Java and C: If you would like to interface with an existing C code base, this appendix provides details for including native C code as part of your Java applications.

Appendix D: Web Resources: We close with how to find more information on the Web.

Compiling and
Running Java Applications

A number of development environments are available now, and more are in the process of coming to market. While some of these are graphical in nature, Sun's original Java Developer's Kit (JDK) is based on simple commands entered at the command line. Since the JDK is readily available on the Web, the basics of the JDK are described here in Appendix A. (See Appendix D for where you can look to acquire Sun's JDK.)

The JDK provides a number of tools, including

- a Java compiler
- a Java interpreter
- a tool for running applets without a Java-enabled browser
- a tool to generate API documentation for your classes automatically

There's also a Java language debugger and class disassembler. In addition, the JDK includes a tool for creating C-style header files. (For a look at this tool, see Appendix C, where we review how to allow Java classes to interact with C programs.)

■ IMPORTANT ENVIRONMENT VARIABLES

First, you should make sure your system can find the JDK commands by adding the directory containing the JDK commands to your PATH variable. Also, you need to set a new variable called CLASSPATH. This environment variable should point to the directories where you've compiled your own classes.

■ THE COMPILER

The compiler is executed using the command javac. You pass javac the file name for the class (or classes) you wish to compile. Include the .java extension in the file name. Here's an example:

```
javac Einstein.java
```

Some useful compiler options include -classpath, -d, and -O.

Using the -classpath *path* option tells the compiler where to look for your classes and overrides the CLASSPATH environment variable.

Using the -d *directory* option tells the compiler to place the compiled classes into the specified directory. This is useful when you're creating your own packages.

With the -O option, the compiler will generate inline code for static, final, and private methods. Therefore, your class files may be larger than when you compile without this option. However, because you'll cut down on method lookups, your code will run faster.

The javac command will create separate .class files for each class described in the Java source file you're compiling. Remember that while the file name does not, in general, need to match any of the class names it contains, there is an exception to this rule. If you define a public class, it must be the only public class in the Java source file, and the file name (minus the .java extension) must match the name of the class.

■ THE INTEPRETER

When you want to run your application, you invoke the interpreter using the command `java`, passing it the class you want to execute. Just use the class name—don't append the `.class` file name extension. Here's an example:

```
javac Einstein
```

The interpreter will then execute your class's `main()` routine. (You'll get an error if you try to execute a class from the command line that does not define a `main()` routine that's defined as `public static void`.) Any arguments listed after the class name are passed to the class's `main()` routine as String arguments in its `args[]` String array.

Some useful interpreter options include `-classpath`, `-ms`, `-noasyncgc`, `-verbosegc`, and `-verify`.

As with the compiler, you can use the option `-classpath` *path* to override the CLASSPATH environment variable and tell the interpreter where to look for your classes.

You can use options that allow you to control how much memory is set aside and how it should be used during a session. For example, you can specify how much memory is available for the heap in bytes by specifying `-ms` *amount*, and you can turn off garbage collection (though garbage collection will still occur if the Java runtime environment runs out of memory) by using `-noasyncgc` as an option.

There are a number of verification and debugging options. For example, you can tell the interpreter to let you know when garbage collection has occurred by using the `-verbosegc` option, and you can run the verifier on all code before it's executed by specifying `-verify`.

If you've grouped your classes into packages by using the `package` keyword at the top of your Java source file, Java expects the directory (or directories) containing your classes (as indicated by your CLASSPATH environment variable) to contain subdirectories named after these packages. All of the classes for a particular package should appear in the appropriately named subdirectory. For example, if you've defined a package named `maps` and a class named `Iceland` that is assigned to the `maps` package, you should have a subdirectory named `maps` that contains your compiled class file `Iceland.class`.

■ TESTING APPLETS

Since applets are meant to be run in a Java-enabled Web browser, they don't necessarily have `main()` routines that you can invoke from the command line. Instead, to test applets, you can use a Java-enabled Web browser, or you can execute a JDK command called `applet-viewer`. The `appletviewer` command expects an HTML document (as will the Web browser, of course), so you must create a document that includes the applet class you want to run. For example, you can create a small HTML file named `Einstein.html` like this:

```
<title>From Here to Andromeda</title>
<hr>
<applet code=Einstein.class width=300 height=100>
</applet>
<hr>
<a href="Einstein.java">Look here for the source.</a>
```

You can then invoke the `appletviewer` command like this:

```
appletviewer Einstein.html
```

The `-debug` option allows you to start the applet in the context of the debugger, which, among other things, sends all sorts of useful debugging messages to the standard output.

■ GENERATING DOCUMENTATION

You can generate great-looking documentation by using the `javadoc` command. Just pass `javadoc` the name of your class, and it will automatically generate an HTML document for you that presents your constructors, variables, and methods, including any documentation you've placed between Java's `/**` and `*/` delimiters.

You can place tags that start with @ between these special comment delimiters that `javadoc` knows how to work with. For example, `@see classname` generates a hyperlink to the referenced class. `@version` and `@author` add special entries for the class version and author name.

Additional tags include `@parameter`, `@return`, and `@exception`, which add special sections to the HTML file that `javadoc` generates. Here's an example of some tags in action:

```
/**
 * Einstein knows a thing or two about time.
 *
 * @see           SpaceShip
 * @exception     WarpSpeed
 * @version       1.0 30 Dec 1995
 * @author        Barry Boone
 */
class Einstein {
        ...
}
```

In addition to passing individual file names to `javadoc`, you can also pass a package name to document an entire package at once.

Appendix **B**

Java Source Code

Appendix B presents the complete source code for six applications discussed throughout this book: Einstein, TownHall, Pendulum, FileBrowser, JavaWalker, and JavaTalker. Applications that were presented in full in the chapters are not reproduced here, including, for example, PlanetaryScale, Escape, and many other code snippets.

■ EINSTEIN

This application was discussed in Chapter 9. It allows the user to perform calculations based on Einstein's equations for time dilation when moving at extremely high speeds.

```
/*
 * Einstein -- Performs calculations concerning time dilation.
 *
 * Tell Einstein what fraction of the speed of light you're
 * traveling to the Andromeda galaxy, and Einstein tells you
 * how long the trip will appear to you, taking relativistic
 * effects (i.e., time dilation) into account.
 */
```

```java
class Einstein {
    static public void main(String[] args) {
        Galaxy      destination = new Andromeda();
        double      distanceLightYears = destination.getDistance();
        SpaceShip   enterprise;
        double      time;

        showInstructions();
        try {
            enterprise = new SpaceShip(getPercentC());
            time = enterprise.calcTimeDilation(distanceLightYears);
            showResults(time);
            showBackOnEarth(distanceLightYears, enterprise.speed);
        } catch (WarpException e) {
            System.out.println("Sorry, dilithium crystals have not
been invented yet.");
        } catch (Exception e) {
        }
    }
    /** Tell the user how this program works.
     */
    static void showInstructions() {
        System.out.println("Enter your speed as a percentage of the
speed of ");
        System.out.println("light. I will calculate the time required
for you to travel ");
        System.out.println("to the Andromeda galaxy, 2.2 million
light-years away.");
        System.out.println("");
    }

    /** Get input from the user.
     */
    static double getPercentC()
            throws java.io.IOException {
        StringBuffer buffer = new StringBuffer();
        char         c;

        while ((c = (char)System.in.read()) != '\n')
            buffer.append(c);

        return Double.valueOf(buffer.toString()).doubleValue();
    }

    /** Tell the user the results of the calculation.
     */
    static void showResults(double time) {
        int years = getYears(time);
        int days = getDays(time);
        System.out.println("Travel time as you perceive it, ");
        System.out.println("with relativistic effects, is: ");
        System.out.println(years + " years and " + days + " days.");
        System.out.println("");
    }
```

```
/** Show what's happening back on earth.
    */
  static void showBackOnEarth(double distanceLightYears, double
speed) {
    double distanceKm = Light.lightYearToKm(distanceLightYears);
    double elapsed = distanceKm/speed;
    System.out.println("Back on earth, " + getYears(elapsed) +
" years and ");
    System.out.println(getDays(elapsed) + " days would have
elapsed.");
    System.out.println("");
  }

  private static int getYears(double time) {
    return (int)time;  // integer portion
  }

  private static int getDays(double time) {
    return (int)((time - (double)(int)time)* 365.0);
  }
}

/** Light keeps track of C and has utilities to perform
conversions.
   */
class Light {
  public static final double Cm_s = 2.998E8;     // meters/second
  public static final double Ckm_yr = 94544.928E8; // km/year

  public static final double lightYearToKm(double lightYear) {
    return lightYear * Ckm_yr;
  }
}

/** SpaceShip instances maintain a speed and know about
  * time dilation.
  */
class SpaceShip {
  double fraction;    // fraction of the speed of light
  double speed;       // speed in km/yr

  SpaceShip(double percent) {
    fraction = percent/100.0;
    speed = fraction * Light.Ckm_yr;
  }

  /** Determine the time required to travel a distance in the
    * moving time frame, given the speed maintained by this object.
    */
  double calcTimeDilation(double distanceLightYr)
    throws WarpException {

    double distanceKm = Light.lightYearToKm(distanceLightYr);
```

```
        if (fraction > 1.0)
            throw new WarpException();

        return (distanceKm/speed) * Math.sqrt(1.0 -
(fraction*fraction));
    }

}

abstract class Galaxy {
    abstract public double getDistance();
}

class Andromeda extends Galaxy {
    public double getDistance() {
        return 2.2E6; // in light-years
    }
}

class WarpException extends Exception {
}
```

▪ TOWNHALL

This application was discussed in Chapter 11. It simulates a town hall meeting among outspoken citizens.

```
/*
 * TownHall -- An accurate model or social commentary?
 *
 * TownHall runs as an application and illustrates multiple
threads.
 */

import java.lang.*;
import java.util.*;
class SynchronizedQueue extends Vector {
        private int     count;
        private boolean started;
        private boolean waiting;
        private int     writers;

        SynchronizedQueue() {
                count = 0;
                started = false;
        }

        public synchronized void checkIn () {
                started = true;
                count++;
        }
```

```
public synchronized void checkOut () {
        count--;
        notify();
}

public synchronized void enqueue(Object elt) {
        super.addElement(elt);
        notify();
}

public synchronized boolean anyoneLeft() {
        if (!started) return true;
        if (count > 0) return true;
        else return false;
}

public synchronized Object dequeue() {
        Object ret;
        while (anyoneLeft() && (super.elementCount == 0)) {
                try {
                        wait();
                } catch (InterruptedException x) { }
        }
        if (super.elementCount > 0) {
                ret = super.firstElement();
                super.removeElement(ret);
        } else {
                ret = null;
        }
        return ret;
}
}

class Speaker extends Thread {
        int             id;
        int             speech_count;
        SynchronizedQueue my_soapbox;

        static String nouns[] = {
                "dogs", "cats", "elephants", "donkeys", "houses",
"monkeys",
                "cars", "bicycles", "computers", "music", "books" };
        static String ends[] = {
                "outlawed", "banned", "imported", "discouraged",
"sold", "bought",
                "given away", "made mandatory", "encouraged",
"deported", "exported" };

        Speaker(int new_id, int turns, SynchronizedQueue forum) {
                id = new_id;
                speech_count = turns;
                my_soapbox = forum;
        }
```

```
        public void run() {
                int i;
                Random r = new Random();
                my_soapbox.checkIn();
                my_soapbox.enqueue("speaker "+ id +" stepping
                        onto soapbox");
                for (i = 0; i < speech_count; i++) {
                        my_soapbox.enqueue("speaker "+ id +": " +

nouns[Math.abs(r.nextInt())%nouns.length] + " should be " +

ends[Math.abs(r.nextInt())%ends.length]);
                }
                my_soapbox.enqueue("speaker "+ id +" stepping
                        off soapbox");
                my_soapbox.checkOut();
        }
}

class MC extends Thread {
        SynchronizedQueue podium;
        MC(SynchronizedQueue new_forum) {
                podium = new_forum;
        }

        public void run() {
                Object utterance;
                System.out.println("MC here: good morning.");
                utterance = podium.dequeue();
                while (utterance != null) {
                        System.out.println(utterance);
                        utterance = podium.dequeue();
                }

                System.out.println("MC here: good night.");
        }
}

class TownHall {
        static SynchronizedQueue podium;
        static int    num_speakers;

        public static void main(String args[]) {
                num_speakers = 5;
                podium = new SynchronizedQueue();

                Speaker[] contenders = new Speaker[num_speakers];
                MC georgeWill = new MC(podium);

                georgeWill.start();

                for(int i = 0; i < num_speakers; i++) {
                        contenders[i] = new Speaker(i, 10, podium);
                        contenders[i].start();
```

```
            }
            try {
                    georgeWill.join();
            } catch (InterruptedException x) { }
            System.out.println("Town Hall closing.");
        }
    }
```

■ PENDULUM

This application was discussed in Chapter 11. It displays an animation
of a pendulum and allows the user to interact with it.

```
/*
 * Pendulum -- A simulation of a free-swinging weight on a cord.
 *
 * Pendulum can be run as an applet or an application.
 */
import java.awt.*;
import java.applet.Applet;

/** Weight behaves like a weight at the end of the pendulum. */
class Weight {
    public static final Color  WEIGHT_COLOR = Color.blue;
    public static final int    WEIGHT_DIAMETER = 50;
    public static final int    RIGHT = 1;
    public static final int    LEFT  = -1;

    int               xpos;
    int               ypos;

    private   int         dir;        // LEFT or RIGHT
    private   double      fastestSpeed;
    private   int         h;
    private   Pendulum    p;
    private   boolean     reverseOk = true;
    private   double      speed;

    Weight (Pendulum pen) {
        dir     = 0;
        speed   = 0.0;
        xpos    = Cord.CORD_PIVOT_X;
        ypos    = Cord.CORD_PIVOT_Y + 200;
        h       = ypos;
        p       = pen;
    }

    public void swing() {
        double    divisions;
        double    ratio;
        double    theta;
```

```
        // Change the angle to move a little.
        divisions = p.cord.getDivisions();
        theta = p.cord.angle + (speed * (Math.PI/divisions) *
(double)dir);

        // Where are we now?
        xpos = (int)(Math.sin(theta) * (double)p.cord.length) +
      Cord.CORD_PIVOT_X;
        ypos = (int)(Math.cos(theta) * (double)p.cord.length) +
      Cord.CORD_PIVOT_Y;

        // Is it okay to possibly reverse direction?
        if (sign(theta) != sign(p.cord.angle))
            reverseOk = true;

        p.cord.angle = theta;

        if (ypos < h && reverseOk) {
            dir       = -dir;
            reverseOk = false;
        }

        // Adjust the speed to match the height in its swing.
        ratio = (double)(ypos - h)/(double)(p.cord.length +
      Cord.CORD_PIVOT_Y - h);
        speed = newSpeed();
    }
    private double newSpeed() {
        double    ratio;
        ratio = ((double)(ypos - h))/
            ((double)((p.cord.length + Cord.CORD_PIVOT_Y) - h));
        if (ratio < 0.0)
            ratio = 0.0;
        return ((ratio + .1) * fastestSpeed);
    }

/** Set the weight to where the user drags it. */
    public void newPosition(int x, int y) {
        xpos = x;
        ypos = y;

        speed = 0.1;

        if (xpos < Cord.CORD_PIVOT_X)
            dir = RIGHT;
        else
            dir = LEFT;

        p.cord.newLength(xpos, ypos);

        h = ypos;
```

```
        // Don't try to reverse the direction of the pendulum's swing
        // until it has swung back through the center.
        reverseOk = false;

        fastestSpeed = Math.sqrt(2.0 * 10.0 * (double)p.cord.length/
10.0 *

            (1.0 - Math.cos(p.cord.angle)) );
    }

    /** Draw the weight. */
    public void draw(Graphics g) {
        int radius = WEIGHT_DIAMETER/2;
        g.setColor(WEIGHT_COLOR);
        g.fillOval(xpos - radius, ypos - radius,
WEIGHT_DIAMETER, WEIGHT_DIAMETER);
    }

    private int sign(double value) {
        if (value > 0)
            return 1;
        else
            return -1;
    }

}

/** Class cord knows how to behave like a cord in a pendulum. */
class Cord {
    public static final Color  CORD_COLOR    = Color.black;
    public static final int    CORD_PIVOT_X  = 250;
    public static final int    CORD_PIVOT_Y  = 20;
    public static final double MIN_DIVISIONS = 60.0; ;

    public int      length;
    public double   angle;
    public double   fastestSpeed;

    Pendulum        p;

    Cord (Pendulum pen) {
        length  = 10;
        angle   = 0.0;
        p       = pen;
        fastestSpeed = 20.0;
    }

    public void newLength(int x, int y) {
        double len;
        double sqx;
        double sqy;
```

```
        sqx = (double)(CORD_PIVOT_X - x) * (double)(CORD_PIVOT_X -
x);
        sqy = (double)(CORD_PIVOT_Y - y) * (double)(CORD_PIVOT_Y -
y);

        len = Math.sqrt(sqx + sqy);
        length = (int)len;
        newAngle(x);
    }

    /** Calculate the angle between the cord and the vertical. */
    public void newAngle(int x) {
        double opp;

        opp  = (double)(x - CORD_PIVOT_X); // can be negative.
        if (Math.abs(opp) < 1.0)
           angle = 0.0;
        else
           angle = Math.asin(opp/length);
    }

    /** The pendulum moves faster the smaller the cord length. */
    public double getDivisions() {
        if ((double)length < MIN_DIVISIONS)
           return MIN_DIVISIONS;
        else
           return (double)length;
    }

    /** Draw the cord. */
    public void draw(Graphics g) {
        g.setColor(CORD_COLOR);
        g.drawLine(CORD_PIVOT_X, CORD_PIVOT_Y, p.weight.xpos,
p.weight.ypos);
    }

}

/** Controlling class to simulate a pendulum. */
public class Pendulum extends Applet implements Runnable {
    public Cord      cord;
    public Weight    weight;

    private Thread   myThread;
    private boolean  freeze = true;

    public void init () {
        resize (500,300);
        cord   = new Cord(this);
        weight = new Weight(this);
    }
```

```
/** Create a thread and make this thread's target the applet. */
public void start () {
   if (myThread == null) {
      myThread = new Thread(this, "Pendulum");
      myThread.start();
   }
 }

/** Keep on swinging and redrawing the pendulum. */
public void run() {
    while (myThread != null) {

        try {
          myThread.sleep(100);
        } catch (InterruptedException e) {
        }

        if (!freeze)
           weight.swing();
        myRepaint();
    }
}

/** Stop the pendulum from swinging. */
public void stop() {
    myThread.stop();
    myThread = null;
}

/** Draw the pieces of the pendulum. */
public void paint(Graphics g) {
    cord.draw(g);
    weight.draw(g);

    // Draw a little red spot where the pivot is.
    g.setColor(Color.red);
    g.fillOval(Cord.CORD_PIVOT_X - 3, Cord.CORD_PIVOT_Y - 3,
6, 6);
    }

 /** Reset the weight to this position as user drags it around. */
public boolean mouseDrag(Event e, int x, int y) {
    weight.newPosition(x, y);
    return false; // pass this event up the window hierarchy
}

/** Called when the mouse goes down. Stop swinging. */
public boolean mouseDown(Event e, int x, int y) {
    freeze = true;
    return false; // pass this event up the window hierarchy
}
```

```
/** Called when the mouse goes up. Start swinging again. */
public boolean mouseUp(Event e, int x, int y) {
    freeze = false;
    repaint();     // clean up when the user moves the pendulum
    return false; // pass this event up the window hierarchy
}

/** Focus the repaint to the pendulum. */
private void myRepaint() {
    int x;
    int y;
    int w;
    int h;
    int border = Weight.WEIGHT_DIAMETER * 2;

    y = Cord.CORD_PIVOT_Y;
    h = weight.ypos + Weight.WEIGHT_DIAMETER;
    x = (weight.xpos > Cord.CORD_PIVOT_X) ?
            Cord.CORD_PIVOT_X - border : weight.xpos - border;
    w = Math.abs(Cord.CORD_PIVOT_X - weight.xpos) + (border * 2);
    repaint(x, y, w, h);
}

  public static void main(String args[]) {
    Pendulum p = new Pendulum();
    p.init();

    Frame f = new Frame("Pendulum");
    f.add(p);
    f.resize(500,300);
    f.show();

    p.start();
  }
}
```

■ FILEBROWSER

This application was discussed in Chapter 13. It presents a list of files for the user to select for viewing.

```
/*
 * FileBrowser -- A file utility.
 *
 * FileBrowser displays Java source files in a directory and allows
 * the user to view these files.
 *
 * FileBrowser is run as an application.
 */
```

```
import java.io.*;
import java.awt.*;

class FileBrowser {
        public static void main (String args[]) {
                ViewFileBrowser picker = new ViewFileBrowser();
        }
}

class ViewFileBrowser extends Frame {
        static int H_SIZE = 300;
        static int V_SIZE = 400;

        String chosen_file;
        List file_elts;

        public boolean action(Event e, Object arg) {
                if(e.target instanceof Button) {
                        String label = (String) arg;
                        if (label.equals("View")) {
                                FileViewer file_viewer =
                                        new
FileViewer(file_elts.getSelectedItem());
                                file_viewer.show();
                                return true;
                        } else if (label.equals("Cancel")) {
                                dispose();
                                System.exit(0);
                                return true;
                        }
                }
                // default case:
                return false;
        }

        public ViewFileBrowser() {
                super("Choose A File To View");

                String filter_suffix = new String(".java");
                String[] file_list;

                // Get a handle on the current directory
                File cwd = new File(".");
                try {
                        /* Get this directory's list of files */
                        file_list = cwd.list();
                } catch (Exception x) {
                        System.out.println("couldn't open .");
                        return;
                }
```

```java
                    // Create an AWT list to display the files
                    file_elts = new List(file_list.length, false);

                    // Add file names that end with filter_suffix
                    for (int i = 0; i < file_list.length; i++) {
                        if (file_list[i].endsWith(filter_suffix)) {
                                file_elts.addItem(file_list[i]);
                            }
                    }

                    // default-selection is the first item
                    file_elts.select(0);

                    add("Center", file_elts);

                    // Create the OK/Cancel buttons

                    Panel p = new Panel();
                    p.add(new Button("View"));
                    p.add(new Button("Cancel"));
                    add("South", p);

                    pack();
                    resize(H_SIZE, V_SIZE);

                    // Wait for the user to select a file, or cancel
                    show();
        }
}

class FileViewer extends Frame {
        static int H_SIZE = 300;
        static int V_SIZE = 400;

        public boolean action(Event e, Object arg) {
                if(e.target instanceof Button) {
                        // This window has only one button
                        dispose();
                        return true;
                }
                return false;
        }

        public FileViewer(String file_name) {
                String str;
                List text_listing = new List();
                FileInputStream file_stream;

                // Get a stream for this file's contents
                try {
                    file_stream = new FileInputStream(file_name);
```

```
                            } catch (java.io.FileNotFoundException x) {
                                    return;
                            }

                            DataInputStream contents = new
                   DataInputStream(file_stream);

                            // Read each line into the List viewer
                            try {
                                    str = contents.readLine();
                                    if (str == null) {
                                        text_listing.addItem("Empty file");
                                    } else while (str != null) {
                                            text_listing.addItem(str);
                                            str = contents.readLine();
                                    }
                            } catch (java.io.IOException x) {
                                    text_listing.addItem("View interrupted");
                            }

                            add("Center", text_listing);

                            add("South", new Button("Dismiss"));

                            pack();
                            resize(H_SIZE, V_SIZE);
                            // Wait for the user to select a file, or cancel
                            show();
                    }
            }
```

■ JAVAWALKER

This application was discussed in Chapter 13. It allows the user to enter a URL and see where it will lead.

```
    /*
     * JavaWalker -- A simple Web walker.
     *
     * Given a root URL to a document, JavaWalker will recursively
     * visit all URLs it can find in the document and all documents it
     * can reach.
     *
     * JavaWalker can be run stand-alone in the interpreter or as an
     * applet.
     */

    import java.applet.Applet;
    import java.awt.*;
```

```java
import java.util.*;
import java.net.*;
import java.io.*;

public class JavaWalker extends Applet {
    public void init () {
        initStandalone (false);
    }

    public void initStandalone (boolean standalone) {
        setLayout (new GridLayout (1, 1));
        add (new JavaWalkerPanel (this, standalone));
    }

    public static void main (String args[]) {
        Frame f = new Frame ("JavaWalker");
        JavaWalker walker = new JavaWalker ();
        walker.initStandalone (true);

        f.add ("Center", walker);
        f.pack ();
        f.resize (350, f.bounds ().height);
        f.show ();
    }
}

class JavaWalkerPanel extends Panel {
    JavaWalker walker;     // The applet.
    List walkerList;       // The list box showing URL hierarchy.
    Thread walkerThread:   // The thread doing the searching.
    Label status;          // The status box for status messages.
    int urlIndex;          // The index of the current URL.
    Button pause, resume;
    String rootURLStr;
    Label rootLabel;
    TextField rootTextField;
    static final String spaces =
        "                                                ";

    JavaWalkerPanel (JavaWalker myWalker, boolean standalone) {
        walker = myWalker;

        GridBagConstraints endConst = new GridBagConstraints ();
        GridBagLayout gridbag = new GridBagLayout ();
        setLayout (gridbag);

        /* Constraints for the last component in a row.  */
        endConst.weightx = 1.0;
        endConst.fill = GridBagConstraints.HORIZONTAL;
        endConst.gridwidth = GridBagConstraints.REMAINDER;

        /* The applet label.  */
        Label label = new Label ("Java Walker", Label.LEFT);
```

```
        label.setFont (new Font ("Helvetica", Font.ITALIC, 24));
        endConst.insets = new Insets (4, 0, 4, 0);
        gridbag.setConstraints (label, endConst);
        add (label);

        /* The text field for entering the root URL.  */
        add (new Label ("Root:", Label.CENTER));
        rootTextField = new TextField ("");
        gridbag.setConstraints (rootTextField, endConst);
        add (rootTextField);

        /* The button control panel.  */
        Panel p = new Panel ();
        p.add (new Button ("Start"));
        p.add (pause = new Button ("Pause"));
        p.add (resume = new Button ("Resume"));
        if (standalone) {
           /* Provide a way for the user to quit the program.  */
            p.add (new Button ("Close"));
        }
        endConst.insets = new Insets (0, 0, 0, 0);
        gridbag.setConstraints (p, endConst);
        add (p);

        /* The list box displaying the URL hierarchy.  */
        walkerList = new List (8, false);
    walkerList.setFont (new Font ("Helvetica", Font.PLAIN, 10));
        endConst.insets = new Insets (2, 10, 2, 10);
        gridbag.setConstraints (walkerList, endConst);
        add (walkerList);

        /* The label for displaying status messages.  */
        status = new Label ("Enter a URL and click on Start.",
Label.LEFT);
        status.setFont (new Font ("Times", Font.BOLD, 10));
        endConst.insets = new Insets (0, 10, 2, 10);
        gridbag.setConstraints (status, endConst);
        add (status);

        /* Initialize the components.  */
        pause.disable ();
        resume.disable ();
        setRootURL ("http://www.cs.washington.edu");
        rootTextField.setText (rootURLStr);
    }

    public boolean action (Event e, Object arg) {
        /* Handle the various button events. */

        if (e.target instanceof Button) {
            String label = (String) arg;

            if (label.equals ("Close")) {
```

```
                    reportStatus ("Closing.");
                    System.exit (0);
            } else if (label.equals ("Start")) {
                if (walkerThread != null) {
                    walkerThread.stop ();
                }
                walkerList.clear ();
                setRootURL(rootTextField.getText());
                walkerThread = new Thread (new WalkerThread
          (this, rootURL ()));
                walkerThread.start ();
                pause.enable ();
                resume.disable ();
            } else if (label.equals ("Pause")) {
                reportStatus ("Paused.");
                walkerThread.suspend ();
                pause.disable ();
                resume.enable ();
            } else if (label.equals ("Resume")) {
                reportStatus ("Resuming...");
                walkerThread.resume ();
                resume.disable ();
                pause.enable ();
            }
            return true;
        }
        return false;
    }

    public synchronized void reportStatus (String message) {
        status.setText (message);
        getToolkit ().sync ();
    }

    public String rootURL () {
        return rootURLStr;
    }

    public void setRootURL (String url) {
        rootURLStr = url;
    }

    public void addURLs (Queue q, int depth) {
        /* Add these URLs just after the current URL, assuming
           that the current URL referenced to them. */
        String indent = spaces.substring (0, depth);

        for (int i = 0; i < q.size (); i++) {
            walkerList.addItem (indent +
                ((URL) q.element
(i)).toString (), urlIndex + i + 1);
        }
    }
```

```java
    public void setCurrentURL (URL url, int depth) {
        /* Make sure that the current URL is visible and that it is
            roughly centered in the list box.  */
        int rows, vis;

        reportStatus ("Fetching " + url.toString () + ".");
        String spaced = spaces.substring (0, depth) + url;

        urlIndex = -1;
        for (int i = 0; i < walkerList.countItems (); i++) {
            if (spaced.equals (walkerList.getItem (i))) {
                urlIndex = i;
            }
        }
        if (urlIndex < 0) {
            System.out.println ("Failed to find URL in list.");
            urlIndex = walkerList.countItems () - 1;
        }

        rows = walkerList.getRows ();
        vis = Math.max (0, (urlIndex - (rows / 2)));
        walkerList.makeVisible (urlIndex);
        walkerList.makeVisible (urlIndex + (rows / 2) - 1);
        walkerList.select (urlIndex);
    }
}


class WalkerThread implements Runnable {
    Hashtable urlsVisited;        // To keep track of visited URLs.
    JavaWalkerPanel walkerPanel;// A handle to the UI.
    Queue workQ;                  // URLs to visit in FIFO order.
    URL rootURL;                  // The URL we start with.

    public WalkerThread (JavaWalkerPanel panel, String urlStr) {
        try {
            walkerPanel = panel;
            rootURL = new URL (urlStr);
        } catch (MalformedURLException e) {
            System.out.println (e.getMessage ());
        }
        workQ = new Queue ();
        urlsVisited = new Hashtable ();
    }

    public void run () {
        walkTheWeb ();
    }

    public void walkTheWeb () {
        int depth = 0;
        int nextDepth;

        walkerPanel.addURLs (new Queue ().enqueue (rootURL), 0);
```

```java
        workQ.removeAllElements ();        // Reset the work queue.
        workQ.enqueue (new Integer (0));   // Start at depth 0.
        workQ.enqueue (rootURL);           // Start here.

    while (!workQ.isEmpty ()) {
        Object o = workQ.dequeue ();

        if (o instanceof Integer) {
            /* Go down another level in the hierarchy. */
            depth = ((Integer) o).intValue ();
            continue;
        }

        URL url = (URL) o;

        /* Don't revisit documents. */
        if (urlsVisited.containsKey (url.toString ()))
            continue;

        StringBuffer buffer = new StringBuffer ();
        walkerPanel.setCurrentURL (url, depth);

        try {
            DataInputStream stream =
                new DataInputStream (url.openStream ());
            String str;

            while ((str = stream.readLine ()) != null) {
                buffer.append (str);
            }
        } catch (IOException e) {
            System.out.println (e.getMessage ());
        }

        /* Remember that we visited this URL. */
        urlsVisited.put (url.toString (), new Integer (depth));

        /* Parse the URLs in this document. */
        URLParser parser = new URLParser (buffer.toString ());

        walkerPanel.reportStatus ("Parsing " + url.toString ()
+ "...");
        Queue q = parser.parse ();
        walkerPanel.reportStatus ("Parsed " + q.size () + "
URLs.");

        /* Add the parsed URLs to our work queue. We prefix the
        URLs in the queue with the depth in the hierarchy that
            they were found. */
        walkerPanel.addURLs (q, depth + 4);
        workQ.enqueue (new Integer (depth + 4));
        workQ.enqueue (q);
```

```
                        /* Pause for a second so we don't hammer Web servers. */
                        try {
                                Thread.currentThread ().sleep (1000);
                        } catch (InterruptedException e) {
                                System.out.println ("Pause interrupted.");
                        }
                }
        }
}

/*
 * A simple parser that extracts URLs from HTML documents.
 */
class URLParser {
        String contents;
        public URLParser (String data) {
                contents = data;
        }

        public Queue parse () {
                int tag, quote, http, html, last;
                Queue q = new Queue ();
                String href;

                /*
                 * Loop through a lowercase copy of the document searching
                 * for the keywords that correspond to URLs. We determine
                 * the indices of the URL text in the copy, and then
                 * index into the original to extract the correctly cased
                 * URL and place it in the queue.
                 * Note that the parser only recognizes URLs of the form
                 * "http:....html".
                 */
                String text = new String (contents);
                text = text.toLowerCase ();

                try {
                        last = 0;
                        while (last < contents.length ()) {
                                if ((tag = text.indexOf ("<a", last)) < 0)
                                        break;
                                last = tag + 2;
                                while (Character.isSpace (text.charAt (last)))
last++;
                                if (text.startsWith ("href", last)) {
                                        quote = text.indexOf ("\"", last);
                                        http = text.indexOf ("\"http:", last);
                                        if ((http < 0) || (http != quote))
                                                continue;
                                        quote = text.indexOf ("\"", http + 6);
                                        html = text.indexOf (".html\"", http + 6);
                                        if ((html < 0) || (html + 5 != quote)) {
```

```
                        last = http + 6;
                        continue;
                    }
                    href = contents.substring (http + 1, html + 5);
                    q.enqueue (new URL (href));
                    last = html + 6;
                }
            }
        } catch (StringIndexOutOfBoundsException e) {
            System.out.println (e.getMessage () + ": Parse error.");
        } catch (MalformedURLException e) {
            System.out.println (e.getMessage () + ": Bad URL.");
        }
        return q;
    }
}

/*
 * A simple FIFO queue class.
 */
class Queue extends Vector {
    public Queue enqueue (Object o) {
        insertElementAt (o, 0);
        return this;
    }

    public Queue enqueue (Queue q) {
        for (int i = 0; i < q.size (); i++)
            enqueue (q.element (i));
        return this;
    }

    public Object dequeue () {
        Object o = lastElement ();
        removeElementAt (size () - 1);
        return o;
    }

    public Object element (int index) {
        return elementAt (size () - index - 1);
    }
}
```

■ JAVATALKER

This application was discussed in Chapter 13. It allows two people to talk
to each other when they're connected to the Internet.

```
/*
 * JavaTalker -- A simple duplex network talk program.
 *
 * JavaTalker allows two people on different hosts to send messages
 * to one another. To use JavaTalker, one user must first start
 * JavaTalker as a server, and then the second user can use
 * JavaTalker to connect to it. The communication port can optionally
 * be specified on the command line.
 *
 * To start JavaTalker as a server, simply run it in the Java
 * interpreter with the server flag:
 *
 *    % java JavaTalker -server
 *
 * To then connect to the server (on the same host):
 *
 *    % java JavaTalker
 *
 */

import java.applet.Applet;
import java.io.*;
import java.net.*;

public class JavaTalker extends Applet {
    boolean server;         // Whether we initiate or accept
connections.
    int port = 5001;        // The default port.
    Socket sock;            // The communication socket.
    String host = null;     // Name of the remote host.

    public static void main (String args[]) {
        new JavaTalker (args);
    }

    public JavaTalker (String args[]) {
        parseArgs (args);

        if (server) server ();
        else client ();
    }

    public void parseArgs (String args[]) {
        int i = 0;
        while (i < args.length) {
            if (args[i].equals ("-port")) {
                port = Integer.valueOf (args[i + 1]).intValue ();
                i += 2;
```

```
            } else if (args[i].equals ("-server")) {
                server = true;
                i++;
            } else if (i != args.length - 1) {
                System.out.println ("Usage:");
                System.out.println (" (server)  JavaTalker [-port
port] [-server]");
                System.out.println ("  (client)  JavaTalker [-port
port] [hostname]");
                System.exit (0);
            } else {
                host = args[i];
                i++;
            }
        }
    }

    public void busyWait (DataInputStream inStream) {
        /* Currently, Java runtime thread scheduling doesn't lend
           itself to having simultaneous readers and writers on
           sockets...they tend to not notice incoming data.
           So we busy wait.  */

        try {
            while (inStream.available () <= 0) {
                Thread.currentThread ().sleep (100);
            }
        } catch (InterruptedException e) {
            System.out.println (e.getMessage ());
        } catch (IOException e) {
            System.out.println (e.getMessage ());
        }
    }

    public void server () {
        /*
         * As a server, we create a server socket bound to the
         * specified port, wait for a connection, and then spawn
         * the reader and writer threads.
         */
        try {
            InetAddress serverAddr = InetAddress.getByName (null);

            System.out.println ("Waiting for connection on " +
                                serverAddr.getHostName () +
                                " on port " + port + ".");

            ServerSocket serverSock = new ServerSocket (port, 50);
            sock = serverSock.accept ();
            System.out.println ("Accepted connection from " +
                                sock.getInetAddress() .getHostName
() + ".");
```

```
                   new JavaTalkerWriter (this).start ();
                   new JavaTalkerReader (this).start ();
              } catch (IOException e) {
                   System.out.println (e.getMessage () +
                                     "Failed to connect to client.");
              }
         }

         public void client () {
              /*
               * As a client, we create a socket bound to the specified
               * port, connect to the specified host, and then spawn the
               * reader and writer threads.
               */
              try {
                   InetAddress serverAddr = InetAddress.getByName (host);
                   sock = new Socket (serverAddr.getHostName (), port,
true);

                   System.out.println ("Connected to server " +
                                     serverAddr.getHostName () +
                                  " on port " + sock.getPort () + ".");

                   new JavaTalkerWriter (this).start ();
                   new JavaTalkerReader (this).start ();
              } catch (IOException e) {
                   System.out.println (e.getMessage () +
                                     ": Failed to connect to server.");
              }
         }
    }

    /*
     * A JavaTalkerReader takes data entered on standard input and
writes
     * it to a socket.
     */
    class JavaTalkerReader extends Thread {
        JavaTalker talker;

        public JavaTalkerReader (JavaTalker talker) {
            this.talker = talker;
        }

        public synchronized void run () {
            try {
                DataInputStream userIn =
                    new DataInputStream (System.in);
                DataOutputStream remoteOut =
                new DataOutputStream (talker.sock.getOutputStream ());
                while (true) {
```

```
                        talker.busyWait (userIn);
                        remoteOut.writeChars (userIn.readLine () + '\n');
                    }
                } catch (IOException e) {
                    System.out.println (e.getMessage ());
                    System.out.println ("Connection to peer lost.");
                }
            }
        }
    }


    /*
     * A JavaTalkerWriter takes data sent on a socket and prints it to
     * standard output.
     */
    class JavaTalkerWriter extends Thread {
        JavaTalker talker;

        public JavaTalkerWriter (JavaTalker talker) {
            this.talker = talker;
        }
        public synchronized void run () {
            try {
                DataInputStream userIn =
                    new DataInputStream (System.in);

                DataInputStream remoteIn =
                    new DataInputStream (talker.sock.getInputStream ());

                while (true) {
                    talker.busyWait (remoteIn);
                    System.out.println (remoteIn.readLine ());
                }
            } catch (IOException e) {
                System.out.println (e.getMessage ());
                System.out.println ("Connection to peer lost.");
            }
        }
    }
```

Combining Java and C

If you are interested in writing Java applications in stand-alone (non-Web) environments, it is quite possible that you will have existing code you'd like to reuse. Coming from a C background, you may have developed libraries for performing sophisticated math or graphics that you want to use again in your Java applications (at least, until you can re-write them in Java!).

While you lose many of the powerful advantages of Java (such as platform independence, garbage collection, verifiable code, and so on), Java is still a relatively new language. As such, it provides a way to interface with legacy code to take advantage of existing C libraries. Appendix C shows you how to combine Java and C.

■ OVERVIEW

Here's the basic idea. Java and C are different worlds. Java expects classes; C wants structures. Java also expects to load code dynamically and resolve references at runtime. How do you marry these two when they come from such different backgrounds? Luckily, the JDK provides a marriage broker, and it's called `javah`. The `javah` command generates the C header files C expects, as well as a `.c` file that gets compiled with the C source code and helps the two languages connect in the call stack.

In addition, both the Java and C code must meet this marriage broker halfway. Java must declare the C methods it will use in such a way that the Java runtime knows these methods are implemented in another language. The C code must be compiled into a dynamically loadable library. The Java side must also indicate when to load this library.

In addition to `javah`, then, there are some other pieces to the puzzle. These all deal in some way with defining a dynamically loadable library. These pieces are

- the `native` keyword, to identify a method as being implemented in a dynamically loaded library
- a call to `loadLibrary()` (a `static` method in the System class), to load the dynamic library when your Java class is first loaded into the Java runtime
- a C compiler capable of compiling dynamically loadable libraries

■ A SIMPLE EXAMPLE

Here are the basic steps you'll follow to connect C code with Java:

1. Write and compile your Java code.
2. Generate the connecting files.
3. Write and compile your C code into a dynamically loadable library.

After you've completed these three steps, you'll be ready to run.

For a simple example here, we'll reimplement the text-based version of the PlanetaryScale application using a C routine to calculate the astronaut's weight on the moon. Recall that we created an Astronaut class that kept track of an earth weight, and calculated a corresponding moon weight:

```
class Astronaut {
    Double earthWeight;

    Astronaut (double weight) {
        earthWeight = new Double(weight);
    }
    public double moonWeight () {
        return earthWeight.doubleValue() * .166;
    }
}
```

This time, let's implement `moonWeight()` using a C routine. Also, to show how to include arguments, let's pass a conversion value to our C version of `moonWeight()`.

Writing and Compiling Your Java Code

To indicate that a method within a Java class is defined in another language, declare it as `native`, as follows:

```
class Astronaut {
    Double earthWeight;

    Astronaut (double weight) {
        earthWeight = new Double(weight);
    }

    native public double moonWeight (double factor);
    // ... more will follow shortly ...
```

The `native` keyword tells the Java compiler that the implementation for `moonWeight()` exists in another language; hence, you only provide the method name, signature, and return value, if any.

You also need to tell the Java class to load a dynamic library when the class is first loaded into the Java runtime. Recall from Chapter 9 that you can execute code when a class is first loaded by declaring a static initializer, like this:

```
class YourClass {
    static {
        // ... code executed at class load time goes here ...
    }
}
```

To load a dynamic library, use the System class method `loadLibrary()`. If the dynamically loadable C library is to be named "nasa", the rest of Astronaut class definition will look like this:

```
// ... continued from above ...
static {
    System.loadLibrary("nasa");
}
}
```

So far, so good. The Java side now expects to load a dynamic library when the Astronaut class is loaded into the Java runtime. Then, a call to the Astronaut's `moonWeight()` method will look for the appropriate C code in the dynamically loaded library, rather than trying to find the method's implementation in Java.

We'll leave the rest of the code the same, except now when we call `moonWeight()` we'll pass in the conversion factor of .116. (As you may remember, the rest of the application consisted of a class called `PlanetaryScale` that used the Astronaut class.) After you've recompiled, you're ready to build the bridge to the C side of things.

Generating the Connecting Files

There are two connecting files you need to generate. All you need to do to create these two files is to use the JDK command `javah`.

The first file will be a C header file that defines a structure representing the Astronaut class (that is, the class that defines the native method). To run `javah`, pass it the class name without any file extensions, as follows:

```
javah Astronaut
```

This code will generate a file called `Astronaut.h` in the same directory as your class file. This header file includes the instance variables for Astronaut in defining a structure called `ClassAstronaut` (static variables are not accessible from the C function and so would not be included if they were defined):

```
/* DO NOT EDIT THIS FILE - it is machine generated */
#include <native.h>
/* Header for class Astronaut */

#ifndef _Included_Astronaut
#define _Included_Astronaut
struct Hjava_lang_Double;

typedef struct ClassAstronaut {
    struct Hjava_lang_Double *earthWeight;
} ClassAstronaut;
HandleTo(Astronaut);

#ifdef __cplusplus
extern "C" {
#endif
    __declspec(dllexport) double Astronaut_moonWeight(struct
HAstronaut *,double);
#ifdef __cplusplus
}
#endif
#endif
```

This automatically generated file also declares a function prototype for `Astronaut_moonWeight()`. The first parameter is a pointer to the ClassAstronaut structure. This can be mapped to a variable called `this` so that you can access the instance variables from the C function, just as if the C function were part of the object. (The second parameter is what we defined in Java to be the factor for the conversion.)

You're now halfway there with bridging the gap between Java and C. There's one more file you need: a stub C file to connect the Java class and its parallel C structure within the call stack. To generate the stub file, use the `-stubs` option in `javah`, like this:

```
java -stubs Astronaut
```

This code will generate a new C file in the same directory as your Java class:

```
/* DO NOT EDIT THIS FILE - it is machine generated */
#include <StubPreamble.h>

/* Stubs for class Astronaut */
/* SYMBOL: "Astronaut/moonWeight(D)D",
```

```
Java_Astronaut_moonWeight_stub */
__declspec(dllexport) stack_item
*Java_Astronaut_moonWeight_stub(stack_item *_P_,struct execenv
*_EE_) {
        Java8 _t1;
        extern double Astronaut_moonWeight(void *,double);
        Java8 _t0;
        SET_DOUBLE(_t0, _P_,
Astronaut_moonWeight(_P_[0].p,GET_DOUBLE(_t1, _P_+1)));
return _P_ + 2;
}
```

You'll compile this wacky-looking file into the dynamically loadable library when you write your C code in just a moment. This will allow you to execute C from within Java.

Writing and Compiling Your C Code into a Dynamically Loadable Library

Now for the C code. You need to include a header file called StubPreamble.h. You also need to define the C function that you'll call the same way as the function prototype that javah generated. We'll store this in a file named AstroC.c:

```
#include <StubPreamble.h>
#include "Astronaut.h"

double Astronaut_moonWeight(struct Astronaut *this, double factor)
{
    return (this->earthWeight * factor);
}
```

Note that this example

- passes a value from Java to C
- accesses the instance variable of the current Java object
- returns a value back to Java

Now create a dynamically loadable library named "nasa" using Astronaut.c and AstroC.c. Every compiler will have its own unique options for creating a dynamically loadable library, so use the options appropriate in your development environment. (Note that StubPreamble.h can be found in the `include` directory under the top-level `java` directory. Your compiler will need to find this directory to know how to include this header file and the other header files to which `StubPreamble.h` refers.)

Before you run the application, define an environment variable called `LD_LIBRARY_PATH` if you haven't already done so. Java uses this variable to find the directories to look in when it loads dynamic libraries. Make sure you include the directory in `LD_LIBRARY_PATH` where you've defined your own dynamic libraries.

Once you have created your dynamically loadable library, you can execute your Java class in the usual way:

```
java PlanetaryScale
```

And, lo and behold, the correct thing will occur!

Remember, even though some of the C code that `javah` generates automatically looks a little funky, the JDK really hides this from you. To recap:

1. Define your native method.
2. Load the dynamic library when your class is loaded.
3. Generate the connecting files using the JDK tools (`javah` and `javah -stubs`).
4. Write the C function using the same call signature `javah` generated.
5. Compile your dynamic library.

Then run to your heart's content!

Appendix **D**

Web Resources

■ ADDISON-WESLEY

Information concerning *Java Essentials for C and C++ Programmers* is available at Addison-Wesley's Web site. Check out

```
http://www.aw.com/devpress
```

■ JAVA

For the Java Developer's Kit, the latest-breaking Java news, and the full API documentation for Java, take a look at Sun's JavaSoft page at

```
http://www.javasoft.com
```

■ PRODUCTS AND LICENSEES

Many leaders in the software industry have licensed Java. Here are the URLs for seven of them that present information concerning Java at their sites:

```
http://www.netscape.com
http://www.metrowerks.com
http://www.ibm.com
http://www.borland.com
http://www.oracle.com
http://www.macromedia.com
http://www.spyglass.com
```

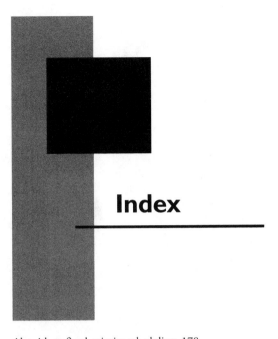

Index